DILEK

by Mollie Zook

assisted by
Ethel Martin Campbell
who typed and edited

Cover Artist: Anna Mae Pellman
Artist: Matilda Nissley

Christian Light Publications
Harrisonburg, Virginia 22801
1983

First printing 5,000
Second printing 3,000

ISBN: 0-87813-521-9

Lithographed in U.S.A.

Preface

Having had the privilege of meeting Hans and Netta Reimer, I personally received their life story from which the true story of Dilek originated.

There are a few fictitious persons and incidents added to make it more complete.

After many trials, Hans and Netta tried to regain the lost truths of the Gospel they had been taught as children in Russia. When communism came into power, their home relationship and former church activities were all destroyed.

Later, however, Hans and Netta with their only child, Dilek, continued to search for the knowledge of God and salvation through His Son Jesus, in spite of hunger, persecution, and many adverse circumstances.

The spark of faith that kindled in Dilek's tender heart burst into a flame that would not be quenched.

Her eager acceptance of the Gospel truths enlightened not only her short life, but also the lives of those who knew her.

Mollie B. Zook

Ask, and it shall be given you; seek, and ye shall find; knock, and it shall be opened unto you: For every one that asketh receiveth; and he that seeketh findeth; and to him that knocketh it shall be opened (Matt. 7:7, 8).

Contents

Chapter		Page
1	Dilek's First Test of Faith	7
2	Not Sorry, Only Hungry	21
3	You Are Wanted in Luzile	37
4	Love Thy Neighbor	53
5	Lessons on Trust	69
6	Another Move	89
7	Dilek Sows	107
8	Answered Prayer	123
9	Reunited	135
10	In Search of Fellowship	151
11	Lothar Returns	163
12	Rejoicing in Heaven	183

Chapter 1

Dilek's First Test of Faith

Dilek's* eyes were open wide with longing as she watched Grandma skin the small hedgehog. The ever-present gnawing hunger grew stronger by the minute. There would finally be something to still the empty aching when Grandma had the hedgehog prepared.

"When can we eat, Grandma?" Dilek asked eagerly, as though she had not asked a dozen times before.

*(pronounced DEE lek)

7

"You must try to be patient, Dilek. See, it is hard to skin the mean little thing with all these needles. As soon as I get its belly opened, it will not take long," Grandma answered a bit sharper than she had intended.

"Ouch!" Grandma winched as she touched a quill in an effort to unfurl the prickly skin. Turning the sharp quills carefully outward, the fatty flesh was exposed at last.

"I'm hungry, Grandma," Dilek whined persistently. "Do you have to cook it first?"

"Of course, Child," Grandma answered more warmly. She felt the same pangs in her stomach, a gnawing hunger that had not been satisfied for so very long.

Grandma tried to brush aside the thought of the ache. How she yearned to feed not only Dilek with more nourishing food than the thin, fatty soup of the hedgehog, but also Dilek's mother. Yet, she was grateful. Had she not been successful in catching the animal, there would not have been anything to eat

8

tonight except the allotted slice of dry black bread.

"I would gladly give them all of it," Grandma murmured to herself, "but I must keep up my strength in order to properly care for them."

When Grandma finished dressing the small animal, she rinsed the carcass and dropped it into a pot of boiling water. With a stick she poked at the fire, adding the dried grass and a few sticks that Dilek had gathered earlier in the day.

"Not too fast. Eat slowly," Grandma warned as Dilek started to gulp the soup. "You will feel better and get more benefit from your food, if you will take longer to eat it."

Having satisfied Dilek with a bowl of the hot soup, Grandma dipped out a bowlful and carried it to Dilek's mother, who lay very still on her mattress of grass. Removing the cloth that shaded the sick woman's head, she offered a spoonful of soup, saying, "Are you awake, Netta? Here, take a sip of warm soup."

The sick woman stirred slightly, but

turned her head away when she realized what Grandma wanted.

"Give my share to Dilek," Netta said, her voice scarcely above a whisper. "I will die anyway." A faint groan escaped the feverish lips. She closed her eyes again.

"No! Please, Netta!" The older woman pleaded, "You must eat to get well. For Dilek's sake, and — and for Hans."

Grandma forced a few drops of soup between the parched lips. Patiently, she fed her daughter until almost half of the bowl of soup was gone. Netta refused to eat more, but took a little water.

Dilek had been near enough to hear Mama say the word *die*. She sprang to her side, grasping the thin hand that lay so lifeless on the damp bed of grass.

"Mama, oh Mama," she sobbed. "You must not die. Please eat. You may have my soup too."

The child forgot her own hunger in the fear of death. At her tender age, Dilek had known of many deaths. "They took Papa away," she sobbed brokenly, "and now — oh, Papa! Why don't you come

10

home to Mama? Then Mama would get well."

For some time, Dilek's body shook with sobs. Finally, Netta reached out to touch her. "Don't cry, Dilek. It will be all right. God will take care of —" Netta's voice trembled with weak emotion. Then all was quiet as Netta settled back into unconsciousness.

Dilek was deeply touched. Mama did not talk to her very much anymore. She never opened her eyes when Dilek spoke. Dilek thought her heart would break if she could not confide in someone. She ran to the rubbish heap that divided their tent from Lothar's and called to him.

"Oh, Lothar. Mama is so sick. She, she —" Dilek gasped with a fresh burst of tears.

"What is wrong?" Lothar asked with concern. "Don't cry, Dilek, for Tussy says it takes energy to cry, and we do not have any extra energy."

"Mama says she is going to die. Oh, Lothar, ask God to spare her and make her well again! Grandma says it's her leg

11

that's bad."

"I don't think God can help, Dilek," Lothar said sadly. "Or He would have helped and not let sister Ilsa die. We needed her, too, when the officer took Mama to work in the grain fields for the government."

Lothar brushed a tear from his cheek with the shred that was left of his shirt sleeve. "They took Papa too, and Tussy and I — we —. No! Dilek, God does not care and He cannot help," Lothar added bitterly.

"Yes, Lothar, He can," Dilek insisted with a determined shake of her head. "I'm sure, for Mama said it will be all right, and that God cares. I'm going to ask Him to make Mama well and to bring my papa home. So there, Lothar!" Dilek stamped her foot defiantly.

Lothar's lack of faith brought to Dilek a strong determination to maintain her faith in God. God could make Mama well again, she thought. She had confidence in her heart that He would.

Dilek did not want to stay any longer to

hear Lothar complain and condemn. Without saying anything more she ran back to the hovel they called home. Nestling up close to Mama on her damp bed of grass, Dilek fell asleep while whispering to God about her sorrows.

Grandma worked long into the night, heating water and applying hot packs to Netta's red, swollen leg.

"Not tonight," Netta moaned. "The heat makes my leg ache all the more. I will be gone by morning. Take care of Dilek."

Netta stretched her bad leg in an effort to relieve the pain. She moaned again, then tried to put more strength into her voice so Grandma could hear. "Write to Hans, if a letter comes. But do not write that I died — so he will come for Dilek."

Exhausted, Netta sank down. Clutching at her throat with a thin hand, she gasped for breath, coughed, and then lay motionless. Grandma leaned close to catch her breathing. For a moment, she feared death had indeed come to claim the life of her sick, starving daughter.

"Mama," Netta whispered after a long wait, focusing her glassy eyes on Grandma. "Please teach Dilek about God. Find a church. Learn more. Tell Hans — tell —" a tear slid down Netta's wan cheek. Waiting a long moment to compose herself and to catch her breath, she continued, "Tell Hans that I — I found the Lord. I want him to seek. Tell —"

Netta could not finish. Again she fainted.

The next morning, Lothar waited anxiously for Dilek at the rubbish divide. It was their usual time to fetch water from the canals before the sun rose too high above the Steppes. He hesitated to call. Had her mama died in the night? Why was Dilek so long in coming?

"There you are. Ready to go for water?" Lothar asked, twirling his bucket uneasily.

"Sure," Dilek answered soberly.

"Did she — is — is your mama —?" Lothar asked haltingly. He did not want to ask the blunt, awful question that lay on his heart.

14

"Mama is still sleeping. She didn't die, Lothar." Dilek was triumphant. She skipped ahead, swinging the wire-handled bucket. Halting, she turned to face Lothar. "You see, I asked God to help us and not to let her die. And He did hear me, Lothar."

"Maybe she didn't die last night, but—" Lothar did not have the heart to tell Dilek that Tussy had said there was little hope that Dilek's mama would live. It was certain that blood poisoning had set in her leg. Already she was in a coma. There were no doctors to call. Even Grandma thought the end was near.

"I want to find some tea for Mama, if I can. Grandma said if she only had some tea for her, it would help," Dilek said hopefully.

"Where would you find tea in this desert, Dilek? Nothing grows around here unless it is irrigated by the canals."

"I will try to find some along the canals, of course." Dilek sighed, too weary to express the assurance she felt, for Lothar always doubted any possibility for which

15

she hoped.

The children's steps lagged before they reached the canal. Any exertion soon weakened their starving bodies. After filling their pails, they sat on the sandy bank to rest.

"Good morning, children. You are out early," Frau Ludwig greeted them cheerfully. She had come from the village to fetch water too. Letting her pail down into the water, she asked, "How is your mama, Dilek? I hear she has a sore leg."

"Mama is so very sick, Frau Ludwig," Dilek said sadly. "But God will make her well, won't He?" Dilek nodded her head assuredly.

"Tussy says she has blood poisoning," Lothar interrupted. "And she is going to —"

"That's too bad, Dilek," Frau Ludwig sympathized, stroking Dilek's matted curls. "Perhaps I should send Frau Cidney to look at the bad leg. She would know what to do."

"Please do, Frau Ludwig. Grandma says she needs tea and more rations to get

16

well. Do you think I can find tea growing along the canals?"

"Your grandma is right. We all need more rations," Frau Ludwig mused in an undertone. Looking about her to make sure no one would see, she pulled a small parcel from under her flowing garment and handed it to Dilek.

"Just a bit of tea for your mama," Frau Ludwig whispered. "Hurry home now, so your grandma can fix it."

The children started off at once. Soon they met Grandma gathering dried grass and sticks. "Frau Ludwig was at the canal, and she gave me some tea for Mama," Dilek whispered, handing over the parcel.

Grandma hurried home with her small bundle of sticks and dried grass. She was eager to fix hot tea for Netta.

Late that evening, Frau Cidney walked in. She examined Netta's infected leg and pronounced it a bad case of blood poisoning. "There is not much hope that she will recover," Frau Cidney told Grandma, "but we will do what we can."

Instead of applying hot packs, Frau Cidney recommended wet, cold packs. "This leg has so much heat in it, I think the cold packs will help to cool it, at least."

Frau Cidney forced a few drops of tea between Netta's lips. "We must get her to drink more fluids, if possible. Please fix a cup of tea for yourself, Grandma. I know you need it. Then get some rest tonight. I will take care of Netta." Each command was given gently, but firmly.

"We cannot thank you enough," said Grandma, tears blurring her eyes. "How did you manage to get the extra rations?"

"One must not ask questions, Grandma. The Lord takes care of his own. I have a question for you though." Frau Cidney turned to face Grandma and Dilek, who were sipping the delicious tea, making it last as long as possible. "How did Netta get such a bad infection?"

"She was working for the government and scratched her foot with a fork while threshing wheat. At first she thought it was only a minor scratch. But working in the dust caused it to become infected. We had no ointment for treatment. It finally got so bad she could no longer work."

"That's terrible. Did they bring her home?"

"No. That's why her leg got worse. She started to walk home using a stick as a crutch. The last three miles she crawled on hands and knees. I don't know how she found her way. Her temperature went so high she was delirious at times."

Slowly, Netta improved. Frau Cidney suggested they move her into the village, in the hopes she would receive medical care. The ride made Netta very ill and no medical aid was available. Netta begged to return to Grandma and Dilek.

Netta continued to gain strength under Frau Cidney's care. Her request to return to her family was finally granted. Netta soon learned, however, that Dilek had become spoiled and arrogant in her absence.

Chapter 2

Not Sorry, Only Hungry

"It is time to go for water," Grandma told Dilek the second time. "I think Lothar is waiting."

"Let him wait!" Dilek retorted crossly. She continued to swing her make-believe doll.

"Dilek!" Mama said sternly.

"I don't want to go for water," Dilek pouted, stamping her foot. "I'm tired and the sun is hot."

"Come here, Dilek," Mama said in a

21

kind, firm voice.

Dilek began to walk away, ignoring what Mama had said.

"I said come!" Mama called again.

Dilek turned and shuffled back to where Mama lay on her grass bed.

"Dilek, your disobedience and disrespect to Grandma makes me very sad. You know you are not to talk back to her, but go when she tells you. You must tell her you are sorry. Then go with Lothar. He has called for you several times. Remember, Dilek, Grandma gets tired too. And God is not pleased when you disobey. Now go and please be a good girl."

"Dilek is still so young, Netta, and tires easily with so little nourishment for strength," Grandma defended Dilek as soon as she was out of hearing.

"True, Grandma, but we don't have an easy life. It is better for Dilek to learn to do her share. We don't want to spoil her because things are hard. Our circumstances may change. We don't know." Netta's thoughts began to wander. She thought of her girlhood days, and of the

22

home she and Hans had had to leave. How happy they had been! They had not prepared to live and work like slaves.

"Come, Dilek," Lothar called, turning to wait for her.

Dilek was in no hurry. She still wore an unbecoming pout and lagged behind, dragging her feet slowly through the sand.

Usually Dilek kept up some childish chatter. Now she was quiet and sullen. Lothar could not understand. He tried to arouse her out of her sulky mood.

"Let's look for berries this morning," Lothar suggested. "Then if we hurry and fetch water, we can play *Follow Me, Alleys* when we get back."

"I don't want to look for berries, or bring any to Grandma or Mama," Dilek said sourly.

"Why, Dilek! Please let's hurry so we will get home before the sun gets hot." Lothar was at a loss as to what to do to cheer up his friend and playmate.

"Listen, Dilek, I wanted you to tell me about God this morning. I will listen now." Lothar coaxed pleasantly.

"No, Lothar. You don't believe when I tell you about God. And I don't think He loves me anymore. I am tired and hungry, and I don't think He cares. Mama says He does, but I can't, can't believe. O, Lothar, I am so bad." Dilek burst into tears.

"Didn't you say that God can make us good?" Lothar asked in surprise.

"Yes, but Mama says you must be sorry for being bad. I am not sorry, Lothar; only hungry," Dilek cried bitterly.

"Please, Dilek. I wanted you to teach me about God. We could ask Him to help us. Then we would not be so hungry all the time. I wanted you to pray that He might send me another shirt too. I need one. And—"

"I can't pray when I am bad, Lothar. And I don't know if God can send new clothes or more rations."

"He helped your mama when she was sick and you asked Him. She didn't die," Lothar challenged.

"I'm still not sure if God can do those things. I would have to ask Mama, and I

24

don't want to right now."

The children were tired and stopped to rest. However, the sand was getting too hot to rest very long.

"Why don't we look for berries now and gather a few sticks before we fill our pails, so the water will not get so warm before we get home?" Lothar suggested.

"I am thirsty and hot right now," Dilek grumbled. "I want to get water first."

Not wishing to upset Dilek more, Lothar complied with her wishes.

"Let's splash some water over our legs, Lothar. That will cool us," Dilek said, splashing water from her pail over her legs.

"We are not to waste any water, Dilek. We could be punished if we do," Lothar whispered fearfully.

"I am not afraid," boasted Dilek. "I don't care if they punish me. I'll just slide down the bank and hang my feet into the water. Then it will not be wasted."

"No, no, Dilek! It's against the law! Please don't!"

Lothar's pleadings were unheeded.

Dilek was soon dangling her feet deep into the water, churning it with swift kicks.

"Oh, Lothar! This feels so good! Come down with me," Dilek called with glee.

"No, Dilek! There is a penalty for those who bathe in the canals. Do come out quickly!"

Dilek was having a grand time. The cool water was so soothing to her burning feet that she decided to cool off all over. The water was shallow enough for wading.

Lothar was white with fright, while Dilek thought only of her pleasure. Neither of them saw the man in uniform until he spoke. "Why are you breaking the law?" he shouted. "Can't you read that sign?" He pointed to one that was planted on the bank close by.

Dilek, too frightened to answer, scrambled up the bank. The officer grabbed her before she reached the top, pulling her out with a jerk.

"It is strictly forbidden to bathe or play in these canals. You will not go unpunished just because you are a child. There is also a fine. Take me to your mama. Now!" The officer emphasized his command with a firm kick.

Dilek screamed and threw herself onto the sand. The officer tightened his grip on her arm and hit her with a stick.

"Get up there, you lazy girl. Save your tears and your voice. They won't get you out of the trouble you are in," he shouted angrily.

The officer started to drag her along, almost wrenching her arm from the socket. Dilek stumbled to her feet, trying to keep up with his swift pace.

Lothar, like one that had wings on his feet, sprang up and fled toward home. His breath came in short, painful gasps, as he flung himself on the grass pad inside his hovel home, unable to speak.

"The officer! He's coming!" he finally gasped. "Dilek — if only she had listened."

"What is it, Lothar? Tell me quickly! We must go tell her mama," Tussy shrieked with fear. She grabbed Lothar and shoved him to his feet.

Lothar told his sad story in short, convulsive spurts. Netta knew there was trouble ahead. "Perhaps you had better go to meet them," she suggested to Grandma.

Grandma went at once to meet the officer and Dilek, who were now approaching the camp. However, he would not speak or release Dilek until he had dragged her into the hovel where Netta lay.

"You sent this child to the canals, unaccompanied by an adult," he hissed, pointing a finger at Netta. "There is positively no bathing allowed in the canals. That is where I found your daughter."

Netta made no excuses. The officer could surely see, without her saying so, that she was unable to carry water. But there was no pity in the hard, piercing eyes of the officer.

"There is a penalty to pay, you understand," the officer continued, shaking his finger. "You will receive no rations for two weeks. That goes for all three of you."

28

"How can I regain strength to go back to work if we get no rations?" Netta asked feebly, hoping he would reconsider.

The officer did not answer but continued writing the necessary information on a note pad. The rations would be withheld, she knew.

"Reimer, you say? Netta Reimer," the officer mumbled to himself, his frown deepening. "Are you the wife of Hans Reimer?" he demanded, glaring at the sick woman again.

"Yes, Sir," Netta answered, wondering what offense she would be charged with now. She could not imagine how they would exist without rations when they could barely exist with them.

The officer scribbled more on his pad, then asked, "Were you ever bookkeeper at the village of Shretton?"

"Yes, Sir," Netta answered again. She was growing weary from the strain of the questioning.

Without changing the icy tone of his voice, the officer bid them a stiff "Good day," and was gone.

Netta sank deeper into her grass bed and slept from sheer exhaustion. Grandma walked to the canal to look for the bucket Dilek had failed to bring home with water. Dilek, feeling guilty for having brought trouble and hardship to her family, crept over to Lothar in search of comfort.

"Let's play *Alleys* now, Lothar," Dilek coaxed. She was tired of talking about the officer and the punishment that had followed her disobedience. Lothar and Tussy had pried out of her every detail of the officer's visit.

"No rations!" Tussy and Lothar had cried in one voice. "You will all starve for sure!"

"Don't worry, Dilek. I will bring food to you," Lothar promised with more assurance than he felt. Doubling up his fists, he swung them as if to take revenge on an imaginary officer. "I'll show him," he hissed.

Instead of crying, Dilek burst into laughter at Lothar's funny motions. Then she became quiet and serious.

"Mama says God will see us through, and He will, Lothar," Dilek stated with a flourish of her hand, as if to say the discussion was closed.

"I will bring a spoon to make alleys in the sand," Dilek shouted, running home to get one.

"I will use this stick to make my alleys," Lothar explained when Dilek returned. "Tussy does not want me to use our only spoon. She is afraid I might lose it or wear it thin."

With her large spoon, Dilek made long impressions called alleys. She made alleys over sand bridges, across sand mountains, through sand tunnels, and over imaginary rivers. She crisscrossed the alleys, making some of them come to dead end. Lothar would seek out her alleys while she sought his. The one who first found the solution to the other's alleys won the game.

Each tried to surpass the other in making deceptive alleys that would have to be retraced before seeking a through one. Dilek won the first game and Lothar the second. By that time the game had lost its excitement and Lothar suggested they play *Touch-Sticks*.

Lothar brought a bundle of smooth, evenly-cut sticks, a game he had designed. Dumping them in a heap, he handed a thin stick with a pointed end to Dilek. "You go first," he offered.

Dilek fished out two sticks without moving any other. After that, her hand seemed too unsteady to win. Lothar's mood soon matched hers, though the game was not finished. He carefully tied the sticks together for another time.

Lothar accompanied Dilek to the rubbish heap. Her steps lagged from exhaustion. His heart ached deeply for Dilek, yet he did not know how to help. Could he stay alive if he shared his own meager rations? A plan began shaping in his thoughts.

"Dilek," Lothar said before she stepped across the divide. He grasped her dress sleeve to detain her. "Don't worry, Dilek, I will find food somehow."

Dilek turned to face Lothar. She saw he

cared, even though she had not listened to him at the canal. "I am sorry, Lothar, I didn't listen to you. I was so tired and hot and hungry. Now you are offering to—." Dilek hung her head in shame.

"That's all right, Dilek. I said not to worry."

"But Lothar, how? You must not give of your rations."

"Tussy says, 'Do not ask questions.' Maybe the God you talk about will show me a way, Dilek. Please ask Him," Lothar whispered, his lips quivering with emotion.

Dilek was puzzled. She couldn't think of any way Lothar could bring them food, even if God helped him. She only hoped what he had said would come true, for she was very hungry already.

"You should have let me go for water instead of making Dilek go," Grandma chided sadly. "Now the pail is gone and so are our rations. The child was too tired and the day was exceptionally warm. No wonder she was cross."

Netta turned her face to hide the tears

of disappointment from Grandma. She
had been praying all day that God in His
wisdom and love would help them in this
hour of trial and suffering. "You suffered
too," she whispered in prayer, "and were
mocked and scoffed. Dear Lord, strength-
en our faith."

"Let's not worry, Grandma," Netta said
almost cheerfully. "We cannot see ahead,
but God can. This trial may even bring
hidden blessings for us all."

"I'll go out to see if I can find another
hedgehog," Grandma spoke wistfully. "If
only your leg would heal, things might
look different."

After Grandma left, Netta lay thinking. Truly, the load fell on Grandma's
shoulders while she lay there so helpless.
She sat up and began to massage her sore
leg, wincing at the pain it caused, but
refusing to give up. Finally she had some
relief. She thought she could actually feel
more circulation surge through her leg.

Resting again, Netta tried to recall
some Bible verses that might strengthen
her faith. "All things work — work for

what?" She tried to reach back through the years to the time when she had attended Sunday school. Had not the teacher taught them a lesson that contained such a verse? "All things work— oh, yes. All things work for good." She could not remember it all. In faith, she clasped its truth to her heart.

"No matter what adverse events cross our path, God can make it well," she affirmed with a smile.

How Dilek's unfortunate incident could be turned into anything good was beyond human comprehension. It would take a miracle from God. She also could not erase the thought of why the officer had questioned her about the bookkeeping job. Dared she hope? By faith she could leave it in God's hands. He alone could be trusted completely.

Chapter 3

You Are Wanted in Luzile

Grandma came home tired and empty-handed. But the dire necessity for food sent her out again in the early morning hours. The calm freshness of the morning air put more vigor into her hungry, weak body. She was rewarded by catching a hedgehog. This time, though, there was not even the allotted slice of black bread to be served with the thin soup.

Grandma was shocked to come home

and find Netta hobbling around with her stick crutch. She had started a fire, so strong was her faith that Grandma would bring something home to eat.

"You will make your leg sore again, Netta," Grandma fussed as she stewed the young hedgehog. "Don't you remember that Frau Cidney warned you about putting your weight on it too soon?"

"I will try not to overdo, Grandma," Netta said weakly. "But I have been massaging my leg. I feel a little exercise might do it some good, if I am careful."

Dilek was delighted to have Mama up again. But her joy vanished when she realized anew how necessary it was for Mama to have bread to regain her strength.

Tearfully, Dilek repented at Mama's knees. "I'm so sorry, Mama. If the officer had only taken away my rations, it would not be so bad. It was not you or Grandma that disobeyed." Dilek's body shook with sobs as she hid her face in Mama's dress.

"I am sorry too, Dilek," Mama said kindly, stroking the matted hair that had

38

been neglected too long. "Not only about the rations, but that you didn't listen and were cross that morning. It never pays to act according to our feelings when we are out of sorts, dear."

Mama waited until Dilek's sobs were subdued, then raised her head and wiped away her tears. "Dilek, if we are truly sorry and ask God to forgive us, He will."

"I have asked Him," Dilek said simply. "I told Lothar that I am sorry too."

Netta knew Dilek's repentance came from a sincere heart. She wanted to teach her to trust also. "I have been thinking, Dilek, of some verses we learned from the Bible when I went to Sunday school. Sometimes God uses other people to teach us lessons. He can use our sad experiences and turn them into blessing. This trial might turn out for our good after all."

Dilek trusted what Mama said would be true. "I wish we could have Sunday school, Mama, and learn Bible verses too." Dilek spoke wistfully, her blue eyes looking into Mama's.

Netta smiled, drawing Dilek close to herself. "We will pray and keep faith that God in His own time will be able to bring it about."

Lothar missed Dilek when he went to the canals for water. Grandma insisted on doing that work herself, always going early in hope of bring home some food. She was empty-handed when she returned the third day. Again, there was no food.

Lothar tried to get Dilek's attention when he came back from the canals. He hoped she wanted to come out to play. But Dilek was not in a mood for active play. She cuddled Linny, her stick doll, to bring her comfort. She could pour out her troubles to Linny, and the doll would not make fun of her like Lothar did at times.

"And remember," she whispered to Linny, as she wrapped rags around the doll, "always obey, and do not be cross or bad, for an officer can pop out of the sand banks, just so!" She snapped her fingers in demonstration.

Lothar never cared to play with dolls.

40

He considered himself to be the man of the family, though he was only nine and his sister Tussy was twelve. Being two years older than Dilek, he thought dolls were for sissies.

By noon Dilek's stomack craved for something to fill the empty hurt. She had to check herself from running to Lothar to ask for just one bite of bread. She knew it would not be nice to beg for part of their rations when she deserved to be punished for being naughty. Lifting the ragged blanket in which she had wrapped Linny, she chewed on the end of the stick that served as her doll.

"At least I can pretend I have something to eat," she decided. Then she walked to the water pail to fill up with water.

Grandma had to go to the canals more often now, for they all drank more water in an effort to lessen the emptiness that gnawed within. They also went to bed early, for in sleep the body did not realize its suffering.

Dilek tried to stay quiet and not use up energy. Mama was lying down with her

41

eyes closed. Dilek knew she was praying. She lay down close to Mama and prayed too. God was their only hope! He would in some way provide.

The evening shadows were lengthening and Dilek's hunger became urgent. Yet she dared not ask Mama for food, for there was none.

"Was that Lothar?" Dilek sat up and listened. Someone had called softly. There it was again! "It must be Lothar." Dilek hurried out to meet him.

"Lothar! Oh, Lothar! Where did you get such a huge turnip?" Dilek gasped, afraid to believe her own eyes.

Lothar put a finger to his lips, motioning to her to be quiet. "Remember, Dilek, I said to ask no questions," he whispered close to her ear.

"Lothar, do you really mean we can have it?" Dilek asked with widening eyes, as Lothar handed it to her.

"You may have that and this," Lothar laughed nervously, pulling three slices of black bread from under his shirt.

"Thank you, thank you, Lothar," Dilek

cried softly, giving Lothar a quick hug.

Lothar was deeply touched. Dilek's hot tear had fallen on his cheek, a tear of gratefulness, he knew. He turned quickly to go, before Dilek would see the tears that stung his own eyes.

"It's nothing, Dilek," he called back. "I'm glad I could."

Dilek stepped closer, detaining him with her hand. "Lothar, it is something. It is much when you are so hungry! You— didn't give us bread from your own rations, Lothar?"

Lothar only shook his head *no* and jumped across the rubbish heap divide.

Dilek carried the large turnip to Mama. "See what Lothar brought us," she said. "He told me not to ask any questions. Oh, isn't it beautiful? And isn't Lothar good?"

Tears came to Netta's eyes. She hoped Lothar had not stolen the turnip. But, truly, would it be stealing? She had to wonder. When she had worked for the government for less than a satisfying ration, she often had carried home a few

43

handfuls of wheat in a hidden pocket so they might have a little more nourishment. She had salvaged little by little, grain by grain, when the guard was not looking. The grain that had fallen on the ground at the bagger would surely have been swept away had someone not taken it.

Grandma did not have to cook the turnip. It was eaten skin and all. Not even a strand of root remained. Grandma, Mama, and small daughter went to bed with thankful hearts and satisfied stomachs. God had indeed provided!

"I want to tell you a story, Dilek," Mama whispered before they went to sleep. "It's a Bible story about how the ravens fed one of the prophets in the wilderness. He, too, was hungry and had no food. God sent ravens to carry food to him."

"I like that story," Dilek smiled brightly when Netta had finished. "Tomorrow I will tell Lothar he was the raven God sent to feed us."

The whole village turned out to watch

44

the approaching wagon. The two mules that were hitched to the wagon plodded slowly down the sandy trail, coming closer to the jumbled group of hovels and tents.

To the children, it was almost as fascinating as a circus. To the women, it could mean more persecution or bad news. It was seldom that anything good came their way. Fear shone silently from every eye.

When the wagon stopped in front of the Reimer's hovel, Netta recognized the officer that had brought Dilek home from the canals that awful day. A woman accompanied him. A shudder rent through her thin, weak frame, as the two alighted from the wagon and walked toward the tent. "Was she to be further punished for Dilek's offense?"

Netta noticed the woman wore a badge and had the same heartless look of the other officer. She sometimes wondered if any of them had any feelings.

"You are Frau Reimer," the lady officer stated, rather than asked. The stern look she gave Netta penetrated so that Netta shivered visibly.

"I am, Madam," Netta replied.

"You are wanted at the Village of Luzile. We have come for you. You will have thirty minutes to get ready. Take only the most essential items."

Netta's thoughts were in a turmoil. What did they want with her at Luzile? They had not mentioned Grandma and Dilek.

"These go too," she stated, taking hold of Dilek.

The officer looked with disdain at Grandma. "She is old and—" Then her gaze turned to Dilek, clinging to Netta in fright.

"I need Grandma to take care of my little girl if I am to work," Netta said weakly.

The lady officer's look of doubt focused on Grandma for a long moment. Netta's heart quaked. She could not part with Dilek or Grandma. "Dear Lord, spare me this trial," she prayed silently.

"All right. Hurry! You have very little

time," she hissed grudgingly. Having given orders, the two returned to the wagon to wait.

Grandma threw the few utensils into the cooking pot, then stuffed some clothes into the water pail. She knew Netta was not able to help much, not with her crutch and sore leg. Dilek grabbed Linny, but Mama said the make-believe doll could not go.

"I need the bucket to pack wet towels in, Grandma," Netta said, dumping the clothes out. "I might need them if my leg hurts on the way." Grandma grabbed the pile of clothes and tied them with some others she had wrapped inside a blanket. The blanket looked more like a bundle of rags, but it was all the clothes they had.

The truth that they were really moving hit Dilek as she watched the hurried packing. She must see Lothar. Slipping quietly from the hovel, she jumped across the divide.

"Lothar, where are you?" she called softly. "We—we are moving."

Lothar and Tussy both came forward,

wide-eyed, curious, and frightened.

"They have come to take us. We are going far away." Dilek's voice shook.

Lothar stared blankly. The sudden truth would not sink in. "Where?"

"Uh, Luzy—Luzile. Oh. Lothar, where is Luzile?"

"I don't know. Dilek, don't go. Who will tell me about God? I want to know," Lothar said brokenly.

"We must go, Lothar. The officer said so. Maybe sometime you can come too. I'll ask Papa when he comes home."

Dilek's heart was torn. She saw tears welling up in Lothar's eyes. How could she leave him? But surely she must go with Mama. Tussy hid her face in her apron.

"Dilek, Di-lek!" Mama was calling.

Dilek grabbed Lothar's hand. "I am sorry I did not obey—"

"Di-i-lek!" Mama's call was urgent.

"Good-bye," Dilek called as she ran for the wagon.

Lothar threw himself on his bed of grass and cried. Papa was gone. Mama

48

was gone. Sister Ilsa had died. Now they were taking Dilek, his one friend on earth. He and Tussy were alone now. Alone! Life had dealt hard blows to a lad of nine.

It was mid-afternoon when the officer stopped at a village to feed and water the mules. Netta had told them she had no rations to take along. Would they care? Dilek wept from weariness and hunger. Netta's own stomach churned from emptiness, and the pain in her leg was worse since the cramped, rough ride on the wagon bed.

The lady officer stayed with them while the other left. When he returned, he handed a parcel to her. Netta was grateful when she handed them each a piece of bread and some goat's milk. Netta, Grandma, and Dilek closed their eyes for a brief, silent, thank-you prayer before they ate.

"Drink it slowly," Netta warned Dilek in a whisper. "Our tummies are not used to this kind of food. Too much at one time might make us sick."

The good food refreshed them greatly.

49

Dilek slept, in spite of the rough, jolting ride.

Netta's leg throbbed. She had to keep wet packs on it most of the way. At the village, she asked for cold water to wet her rags. To her surprise the lady brought some for her.

Netta thanked the officer warmly. She gave no sign of having heard her, but kept the same stern glare all the way.

When at last they reached the village of Luzile, the officer stopped at an inn. They had to walk almost a block to the basement apartment that was to be their home. Grandma and Dilek made a second trip to bring their belongings. Netta had carried a few things, but it was almost more than she could do to bring herself. How thankful she was that she had massaged and exercised her leg before the move.

The officer unlocked the basement door and pulled it open. "I will come for you at eight on Monday morning. Be ready for work." The officer gave his orders before leaving.

Netta sighed with relief. She looked about the one-room apartment. There was a long crack across the concrete floor. The room smelled musty from dampness. She hobbled to the window and opened it to air out the room.

"It isn't much," thought Netta. "But it is more than the hovel we left at the Steppes."

There was a small tin stove standing in one corner. She was very grateful for that.

Netta picked up the parcel the lady officer had left. It contained bread. Then she looked over the papers that had been given her to fill out before reporting to work on Monday.

"So, indeed!" Netta chuckled. "I am to be the village bookkeeper."

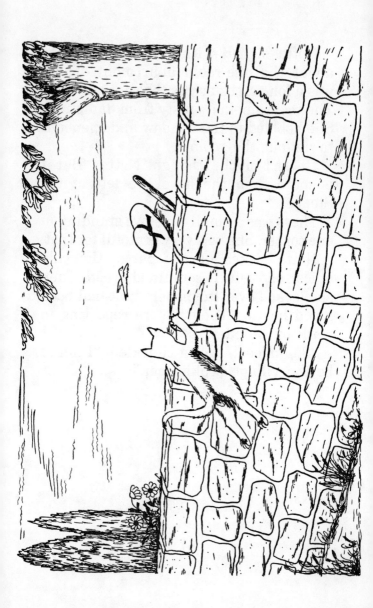

Chapter 4

Love Thy Neighbor

The sunlight filtered through the small basement windows, making cheery, blotchy patterns on the rough concrete walls. When Netta awoke, she thought, "What a warm welcome to Luzile." "Thank You, God, for Your directing hand and watchful eye over us, and Hans too."

With the aid of her crutch, Netta hobbled up the steps and out into the courtyard to have a look at their surroundings. She was delighted to see a small fenced-in garden, though it looked overgrown with weeds. "Now for some seeds when the weather warms up," she mused, immediately making plans to increase their food rations.

Netta breathed deeply of the fresh morning air as she walked to the far side of the courtyard. "The air is as fresh as the wet dew that dampens my sandals," she thought aloud. "Not stuffy and humid like the Steppes."

A low chicken house was nearly hidden behind some tall bushes. Netta turned and took a quick survey of their outdoor quarters. She thought of many possibilities. "We can have a little bit of heaven back here," she thought, "even if we live in that dark basement."

Netta was still deep in thought with her plans when Dilek called from the basement entrance. Mama held out her hands, inviting her daughter to come.

Dilek fled to Mama as if she feared some officer would suddenly grab her. Everything was so new and strange here.

Mama hugged Dilek. "Isn't it nice out

here? Or at least we can make it so, with some hard work. What do I hear? Listen. Do you hear it too?"

"What is it, Mama?" Dilek strained to hear. "Is it a baby?"

Just then a little yellow kitten came around the corner of the chicken house. He stopped when he spied Dilek; then let out a pleading, "Mee-eow!"

"You dear little kitty," Dilek cried, picking up the kitten. "Are you hungry? May we keep him? Oh, Mama, please?"

Netta's face clouded. How could they possibly feed a kitten? "It might be someone else's, Dilek. We must find out. Maybe if we wait and watch, we will find the owner."

Dilek buried her face in the cat's fur. "Mama, he makes a funny noise inside," she squealed with joy. "The kitty is so soft and cuddly!"

"We will see what we can do," Mama added after some thought. Dilek would need something or someone to play with while she was at work.

Netta was grateful for a few days' rest,

time to prepare for public appearance, and time to help Grandma get things in order at home. They got acquainted with Frau Molott, who lived in the apartment above them. Libby, her four-year-old daughter, became Dilek's friend at once.

Dilek was relieved that the kitten belonged to Libby. Now she could share affection for the kitty with Libby. The kitten also soon learned it was just as accepted at the basement apartment as it was at home.

"Let's name him Spot," Dilek suggested to Libby. Libby readily agreed. "See? He has a pretty spot on his fuzzy face." Dilek stroked him fondly. She treated her new little friend and pet as though they were members of her family.

Netta skimped and saved from her meager earnings. The lump of savings grew slowly. She hoped to have a few chickens in the chicken house, and a goat to eat the weeds in the yard and provide them with milk, a luxury not included in their allotted rations.

The basement apartment took on a new

appearance. Grandma scrubbed the concrete walls and floor, leaving a clean smell. Frau Molott shared a few things to help furnish the room. Dilek was delighted when Grandma made a quilt for her bed from scraps of cloth that Frau Molott shared with them. They now slept on rag-padded mattresses instead of grass. Netta also bought some pillows. The apartment became home to the three.

"It is too nice to go to sleep on," Dilek exclaimed happily, as she snuggled down in the softness of her new bed. All at once she bolted upright, still clinging to the pillow, tears streaming from her eyes.

"What is it, Darling?" Mama thought she must have hurt herself.

"Lothar," she sobbed brokenly. "Lothar is still sleeping on grass."

"Let us pray for Lothar and Tussy," Mama soothed, wiping Dilek's tears. "God knows and understands. He will help in His time. You believe He can, don't you, Dilek?"

Dilek nodded and tried to choke back

her sobs. Netta realized how much Dilek must miss her friends from the Steppes.

Though Dilek missed Lothar greatly, she did enjoy Libby and Spot and the added comforts they now had. She helped Grandma carry water from the village well, and did other jobs willingly. Most of her time, however, she spent with Libby and Spot.

Grandma longed for some yarn to knit clothes for Dilek. "She is outgrowing most of her clothes," she told Netta one day. "Perhaps I could get more patches and make a dress from those, like I made the quilt."

"Those needs will come next, Grandma. But first the goat, if I can find one. I think perhaps I have saved enough or nearly so."

Dilek was excited over the prospect of a goat. She dearly loved animals.

"When can we bring the goat, Mama?" Dilek questioned one morning.

"Very soon. I think I know now where we can find one. I must see the man that owns the goats first." Netta smoothed the silken curls that were pressed against her.

"How tall you are growing, Dilek. See how high you come up to me," Mama laughed, holding her hand where Dilek's head had rested against her chest. "No wonder Grandma says your clothes are getting too small."

Dilek spun around on one foot. Catching Mama's hand, she pressed her lips to them. "I love you, Mama. I love Papa, too, and I wish he would come home to see our new house."

"We must do more than wish, Dilek. We must keep on praying for Papa and have faith too." Mama was solemn. "We must not forget others' sufferings and trials just because we have more comforts. I must go to work now. Be good for Grandma and play nicely with Libby. Stay off the streets, for they are dangerous."

Netta gripped the new crutches she had received at the office, and prepared to walk the eight blocks to work. She, too, longed for Hans, or at least for a letter that would indicate he was still alive. It had been so long since she had heard from him, but moving to a different location might have caused the delay. Yet, she had written since. Sometimes her heart almost wavered. Then she would commit herself anew to the Lord in trust. "Someday this too shall pass," she whispered.

"Come in," Frau Molott called kindly in answer to Dilek's knock. "How is Spot this morning?" She smiled, seeing the kitten wrapped in a blanket and cuddled in Dilek's arms. "It is a bit chilly this morning, isn't it?"

"Yes. I wrapped Spot up in my doll blanket. I brought it along to Luzile, but I did not bring my doll. Grandma says I no longer need a doll if I have Spot. He is nicer than a doll anyway, isn't he?"

"I suppose so, Dilek. But why didn't you bring your doll?"

"It was only a stick. Lothar made fun of it. I would not have wanted anyone to see it," Dilek confessed, hiding her face in Spot's blanket.

"I'm sure your doll was nice to play with."

"Spot is much nicer, Frau Molott. He can wiggle and purr inside when I cuddle him. I just love him!" Dilek hugged the little kitten too tightly.

"Mee-oow!" Spot struggled to get out of the blanket.

"Oh, I'm sorry! Spot, I didn't mean to hurt you."

"Why don't you and Libby play out front this morning? The air is cool but the sun is warm. Stay off the street, though. You may play in the back yard this afternoon when it's warmer," Frau Molott advised.

The children were content to sit on the front steps and watch the horses and riders go by. They were especially interested to see an occasional motor car come up the street, churning the dust. Dilek had not seen any cars before coming to Luzile.

After awhile Dilek suggested, "Let's play skip-jump on the stone walks." She had been accustomed to forming her own games when she had played with Lothar.

Dilek and Libby were so busy playing in the sunshine they soon forgot all about

61

Spot. They had left him lying in the blanket on the steps. Suddenly Libby saw him run across the street after a bird.

"Look! Spot!" Libby cried, pointing in the direction she had seen him go.

Dilek looked in time to see Spot leap over the stone wall on the other side of the street. In the next instant she heard the shrill, angry cry of a woman. "I'll kill you, you old cat! You! Running over my flower beds!"

Dilek heard an object hit the stone wall with a thud! Spot let out a sharp, piercing howl.

Without a moment's delay, Dilek fled to Spot's defense. Like a young tiger, she bolted across the street, over the stone wall, landing with a crash amid showers of splintered glass. She had landed right in the middle of Frau Chusik's prized, glass-covered hotbed.

Frau Chusik was numbered among the few well-to-do residents of the village. Her late husband had been a high-ranking officer. His death had increased the bitterness of her solitary life. Being proud and haughty, she despised the poor.

Frau Chusik grabbed Dilek by the arm before the child could realize what had happened. She jerked her from the shattered hotbed, not caring that Dilek's legs were cut and bleeding. She shook her until her teeth chattered.

"I will teach you!" she screamed. "I have enough trouble with the cats in this neighborhood, without you trampling my beautiful plants. Come on! I am taking you right to your mama. She will have to answer for this."

Across the street she dragged Dilek, who was crying from fright and frustration. She had not seen Spot and feared this angry woman had indeed killed him.

Grandma gasped in astonishment when she saw Dilek. "What happened to your legs?" Grandma's attention focused on Dilek. She scarcely noticed the haughty, angry neighbor.

Frau Chusik gave no thought to the injury the girl had received. With her eyes flashing at Grandma, she shook Dilek again. "This culprit has been stamping around in my hotbed," she screamed. "And you," she emphasized with a shaking finger close to Grandma's face, "are going to pay every cent of the damage!"

Frau Chusik waited for an answer, expecting Grandma to raise a defense against the charges. She steeled herself against the tirade she anticipated.

But Grandma remained calm, though she was startled by the angry woman's rudeness. Seeing that Grandma was not going to argue, Frau Chusik repeated her charge.

"Every cent! Glass, plants, and all! So there, you ruffian," Frau Chusik hissed through clenched teeth, giving Dilek a push with such force that she spun across the room and would have sprawled on the floor had not Grandma reached out her hand to catch her.

"I am the child's grandmother. Her mama will not be home from work until after seven tonight," Grandma said weakly.

"So she will hear from me tonight!"

Grandma breathed a sign of relief

when Frau Chusik left the room. The atmosphere had grown stifling. Grandma walked to the window and opened it. Then, remembering Dilek's bleeding legs, she prepared to clean and dress the wounds.

"Now we can't have a goat. Oh, Mama," Dilek wept tears of regret. "I am always getting you into trouble. Spot's cry and the angry woman's voice made me forget about not going into the street."

"That may be true, Dilek, but you must be made to remember always to obey. It's dangerous to be in the streets, and it isn't nice to get into other people's yards and flower gardens. I must think of a punishment that will help you to remember to do what Mama tells you." Netta spoke firmly.

It would have been easier to tell Dilek she was not as much at fault as the angry neighbor who had no pity on the poor. But Dilek would have to learn to respect her elders, even if they were rude and greedy. She must also learn to respect another's possessions.

Netta took Dilek to Frau Chusik to tell her she was sorry and to agree to pay the damages. Her heart sank at the price Frau Chusik asked. It was nearly double the cost of repairing the damaged property.

Netta noticed that Frau Chusik took in the crutches at a glance. Yet she never asked about the cause, nor was she softened. A hard glint of hatred shone plainly from her steel gray eyes.

That night, Dilek was nearly asleep when she heard the familiar, pleading Me-eow, at the door. Springing to her feet, she ran to let him in.

"Dilek!" Mama called. "Don't open that door!"

"But, Mama," Dilek gasped, "I haven't seen Spot since she— she— that hateful old woman beat him, and—"

"Dilek!" Mama's voice was stern. "Don't let me hear you speak disrespectfully of Frau Chusik or anyone else. Just because she wasn't as kind as she might have been, you have no reason not to be forgiving. Don't forget that."

"But, Spot," Dilek reached for the door

again.

"Come here, Dilek," Mama continued. "I have decided you are not to play with Spot, or feed him, or let him in our house for two weeks. This will be your punishment. If Frau Molott or Grandma report that you disobey, there will be an even greater punishment. Now, go back to bed."

"Mama," Dilek pleaded, choking back the tears. "Please look after Spot. He may be hurt or hungry."

"I'm sure he isn't hurt badly or he wouldn't have been able to come home." Mama was not going to waver.

Netta lay awake long into the night. Frau Chusik had not only demanded all the money she had saved, but also all she would be able to save in another month or two. It wouldn't hurt her to fast again to save on food rations. But Dilek's scrape and the loss of her hard-earned savings were not the only things Netta's thoughts dwelt on. She had finally received a note from Hans. The stamp on it was from Ultimo, the Federal Prison.

Chapter 5

Lessons on Trust

It was a hard day at the office for Netta. She had had a thumping headache all morning. The mayor demanded that some important papers be ready at a set time. Netta thought he seemed more irritable than usual. In addition, the thought that Hans was in prison and perhaps in serious trouble sapped at her strength. By evening she was nearly unstrung.

In a daze, Netta walked home over the rough streets. Inside the basement door, she collapsed in exhaustion on her rag mattress.

Then she saw the visitor. Grandma had her seated on the large cracked crock she had found in the chicken house. With Dilek's quilt draped over it, the seat was quite comfortable.

Netta made efforts to rise, but the stranger remonstrated "No, no. Please don't get up," she said softly, kindly motioning for Netta to remain on her bed. "You are tired, and I will be leaving soon. I have already talked with Grandma here, and she is willing to do some knitting for me, if you don't object."

The stranger paused, smiling at Netta. "She also told me you had saved money to buy a goat. My brother lives on a farm and has goats. I think we can easily arrange for you to have one, using Grandma's knitting money as payment. Good night. I will see you again. Blessings to you."

Netta wanted nothing to eat; she wanted only rest. Grandma brought her a cup of hot tea. Sipping the tea, Netta compared the two most recent visitors. "What a difference it makes when a person has compassion. Tonight this kind lady left us with a warm, comforting atmosphere, while the other—," Netta stilled her thoughts.

Netta felt refreshed the next morning and was ready to listen to what Grandma had to say.

"Look at this box full of mixed yarn pieces the lady brought us." Grandma beamed gratefully. "I shall make many warm garments. The mixed colors won't matter."

"How thoughtful," Netta smiled. "But who is this stranger? How did she come to know about us?"

"She addressed herself to Dilek as Tante* Esta," Grandma explained. "She also told me that everybody calls her Tante Esta and that we should too. She has relatives living in the city, and they have sales for knitted garments. She says that as soon as she receives another sup-

---

*(Translated, means "Aunt.")

ply of yarn, I can start to knit to sell. She will even take care of the transactions." It was obvious that Grandma was excited and enthusiastic about her new friend and her new opportunity.

"Do you think she knew anything about— you know, the happening across the street?"

"She did not mention it, but I do think many people living close by saw or heard of it. When she mentioned the goat, I felt certain she knew all about it."

Tears welled up in Netta's eyes. "Lord, thank You for this lesson on trust. Continue to teach me. Yesterday the way seemed dark, today the sun shines again!"

Netta walked to work that day with a song on her lips and thanksgiving in her heart. "God does care. He knows our needs. And I can be assured He will take care of Hans too, even in prison."

Grandma's needles flew as she knitted garment after garment. Netta helped at night as often as she could. "It is getting late," Netta said one night. "I must get more rest to do my best at the office."

"You go on to bed. I think I can knit for another hour yet," Grandma answered.

Netta would not hear of it. "Your days are long enough. I would rather get up a bit earlier and help you before I go to work."

Dilek had a new knitted dress and sweater. Grandma had blended the colors so beautifully no one would have guessed the garments were made from scraps of yarn.

"You are a real wizard at knitting," Frau Molott said, after seeing the dress that Grandma had made for Dilek. "What would you ask to knit one like it for Libby?"

Grandma only smiled. "Perhaps some day," she answered hesitantly. Frau Molott decided Grandma was not anxious for the job. She spoke no more of it.

During the day Grandma was teaching Dilek to knit. Dilek didn't go out as often because she was not to play with Spot. Now that she was learning to knit, Dilek had an attraction that kept her confined more and more to their apartment.

"We will keep it a secret and surprise Mama," Grandma told Dilek. She knew this would make knitting even more interesting and desirable for her granddaughter.

"It's like playing a game," Dilek laughed.

Netta became suspicious. Dilek was too excited and giggly whenever she came home from work. Her eyes would dance and glitter even though she never spoke of anything special.

"Tomorrow may I play with Spot again?" Dilek asked one evening, when it was time for the ladies to put up their knitting.

"Let's see. It has been two weeks." Netta smiled at the serious face of her daughter. "Really, I guess you could have played with him today, if I had just thought of it."

"Um, well, not today," Dilek murmured, before covering her mouth with her hand and glancing sideways at Grandma. "I—oh, Grandma. Must I wait until tomorrow?" she whispered.

"Do as you please, Child," Grandma said. "You probably won't sleep if you have to wait until morning."

Dilek dug under her mattress, pulled out a parcel, and handed it to Mama. "Something I have made for my Mama!"

Netta unfolded the neatly-knitted scarf. "You didn't knit this, did you, Dilek?"

"I did, Mama. Grandma taught me how. And look here." Dilek squealed with joy, holding up a partly finished dress. "For Libby, Mama. Isn't it pretty?"

"She will need a little help with that," Grandma smiled at Dilek's enthusiasm. "I think she has learned well."

"I am glad you have learned to knit, Dilek. Grandma taught me too, when I was a little girl."

"You must not tell Frau Molott, Mama. I want the dress to be a surprise."

"When Frau Molott asked to have a dress made for Libby, I thought it would be nice if Dilek could make it without charge, because she did so much for us when we moved here. She gave us the patch pieces too, and other things that made our home more pleasant. That is what I should do, isn't it?" Grandma asked.

"Certainly, Grandma. I wouldn't consider payment to have the dress made."

"Remember, Dilek," Mama warned the day the goat arrived, "A goat can do more damage than a cat. You must never untie this goat. Absolutely never!"

"I will never forget," Dilek promised. "She is such a nice Nanny. May I milk her, Mama?"

"I will milk her until she is used to us and her new home," said Mama. "Then perhaps you may learn to milk her when I'm here to help. You may feed her though. The kind man from the farm brought some hay and feed along for her."

Dilek could hardly stay away from the goat. She felt sorry she had to sleep outside. "Couldn't she come inside our house just for the night?" she asked.

"No, Dilek. Certainly not. Animals like to live outdoors. You need not feel sorry

76

for Nanny as long as you take good care of her, feed her, and give her plenty of water."

"Why does she cry then?"

"She is just calling for the other goats she is used to sleeping with. She will soon get used to her home here."

Netta emptied the bag of coins and counted them carefully. "I have saved enough to make the final payment to Frau Chusik. Dilek and I will take it to her before we eat."

Grandma looked up with a questioning frown. "Dilek?"

"She should go along as a last reminder," Netta explained with more calmness than she felt.

"Please, Mama, I don't want to go." Dilek pleaded. "She doesn't like children. Especially not me!"

"We meet all kinds of people and often have to deal with problems that are not pleasant, Dilek. When we face our problems honestly, we can always learn from them. Problems are usually opportunities for growth in disguise. Come." Netta took

77

Dilek's hand as she walked toward the door.

Netta trembled as she walked up the winding stone steps that led to the veranda. Pungent green bushes bordered the walkway, and potted geraniums bloomed profusely on the veranda. Vinca vines and coleus overflowed the flower boxes, while a few late roses adorned the trellises that closed in the west side of the veranda.

Mother and daughter scarcely dared to take in the beauty of the well-kept garden. A thought flashed through Netta's mind. How could a person be so haughty and cold while living among such beauty and grandeur every day? Perhaps Frau Chusik did not recognize God's handiwork and blessings.

Netta had reached for the knocker on the door, when she heard a low groan.

"What's that?" whispered Dilek, frightened.

Another groan and a stifled sob came from behind the bushes near the veranda. A faint "help" was followed by more groans.

Netta crossed the veranda with long strides. It was Frau Chusik's voice, and she was in trouble.

"Can I help?" Netta asked when she saw Frau Chusik doubled over in a heap beside the bushes. She clasped her right ankle with both hands, beads of sweat standing out on her white forehead. Netta saw that her pain was intense.

"Please," Frau Chusik said faintly. "I twisted my ankle and oh, it hurts!" Frau Chusik rocked back and forth, still clutching her ankle. "I must have fainted."

"Do you think you can walk to the house if I help you?" Netta asked kindly.

"I can try, but—"

"Quickly, Dilek, tell Grandma to bring my crutches. Be careful when you cross the street," she added as Dilek fled to do her bidding.

When at last they had Frau Chusik reclining on a couch, Netta applied cold packs to the swollen ankle.

"Are you sure it isn't broken, Frau

79

Chusik? I believe you should see a doctor," Netta said with concern.

"There is no doctor in the village. I don't want to go to the hospital in the city." Frau Chusik winched as Netta applied another cold wet cloth. "Don't you think warm packs would be better?" She bit her lips to keep from crying out in pain.

"I'm afraid not, Frau Chusik. As long as there is heat in the ankle, cold will help reduce the swelling and lower the temperature." Netta was grateful that Frau Chusik no longer used her haughty tone of voice. She kept her gaze fixed on her ankle instead of on Netta.

When at last the severe pain subsided, Frau Chusik dismissed Netta. "I can do very well now. Thank you."

Netta viewed the woman with compassion. "Frau Chusik, I once had a painful leg too. I know the pain can become unbearable, if not given proper attention. I will stay here tonight. No doubt you will need more cold packs before morning, to ease the pain. I can't think of leaving you here alone."

Netta saw Frau Chusik wince, but not from pain. She took several deep breaths, the haughty expression crossed her face, then left. "I would be much obliged, if you will be so kind," she breathed in an undertone.

"Could I fix you some tea or broth, perhaps? You haven't eaten this evening."

"No, I haven't eaten; not at noon either. I slipped when I started in for lunch."

"You mean to say you hurt yourself before lunch? No wonder your ankle was so swollen."

"I was late coming in and must have fainted after the fall. You may fix tea and soup, and fix some for yourself too."

Netta was grateful for the offer. She was feeling weak from hunger, as she had skipped lunch all week.

After eating, Netta came to carry the empty dishes away. "I'm glad I came over, Frau Chusik," she said. "I brought the final payment to cover the damages."

Frau Chusik winced again. She turned her face away. "I can't take any more money. You have helped me, and—."

"That's all right. I don't want any pay to help you. A kind person helped me or I would not be here tonight," Netta said thoughtfully. "I believe God planned this so I could be here to help you at the right time."

A look of pain crossed Frau Chusik's brow. "You may stay to help, but I do not want to hear you mention God again!"

Netta realized she had touched a subject that brought back unpleasant memories to Frau Chusik. After that she was careful not to express herself freely, so as not to offend her.

"I want Dilek to take a bowl of soup to Frau Chusik at noon," Netta told Grandma before she went to work the next day.

"While you don't eat?" Grandma seemed disgusted.

"It doesn't hurt me to do without, Grandma. We will do what we can for her. This may be the only way we have to show her Christ's love. I think she will appreciate it."

"Come in," the voice said, when Dilek

82

knocked at noon.

"I brought some hot soup," Dilek said bluntly, taking the covered bowl to the woman on the couch. "Grandma said to ask how the lady's ankle is."

Frau Chusik smiled. Dilek stared. She had never realized this haughty face could smile.

"It is very kind of you. My leg is still very sore and swollen, but the pain is not as bad as it had been."

"Grandma said Mama won't eat lunch today. Mama said it won't hurt her. She has more to eat now than she did when we lived at the Steppes."

"What did you eat then?" Frau Chusik asked, enjoying the child's candid conversation. She had felt lonely after Netta had left early in the morning.

"Sometimes we had hedgehog soup, if Grandma could catch one. We also had bread, until our rations were taken away."

"When was that?" Frau Chusik asked, finding her young neighbor quite amusing. "Perhaps you could bring me a glass of water too. Would you please?"

Dilek hurried to obey, then explained, "We had to carry water from the canals. One day, I went into the water to cool off, and an officer saw me and took our rations away. I didn't think he was kind, but Mama says God made it come out all right, because then she got work here in the village. But we had to leave Lothar."

"And who is Lothar? Your brother?"

"I don't have a brother, only Papa, and they took him away." Dilek became sad. "I pray God will bring him home, and I know He will."

"But, Lothar. Who is he?"

"My friend back at the Steppes. He and his sister, Tussy, are alone now. I hope Papa will soon come so he can bring them home."

"Did you have soup for lunch?" Frau Chusik frowned, trying to steer Dilek's conversation into another channel.

"Not yet. Grandma said I must come home right away, so I will not get into—" Dilek stopped abruptly, abashed, and not knowing what to say.

84

"Bring me that dish on the cupboard, Dee—Dee— uh, what is your name?"

"Dilek," she answered, bringing the bowl.

"You may have some bon-bons," Frau Chusik said, taking several from the bowl. "And here is something else. Take it to your Grandma." She slipped a coin into Dilek's hand. "Now you had better go eat your lunch. Come again sometime."

Dilek smiled, feeling quite at ease. "I will, maybe. But I will be sure to leave Spot at home," she added soberly.

Dilek turned to go, then thought of the bowl she had brought. "I will take the bowl back, please, or Mama will not have one to eat her supper."

"Sure, take it along. I can't get up to wash it, though. You must excuse me. It is empty, but not clean."

Dilek looked at the bandaged ankle. "Mama had a bad leg, too, and she said she would die. I prayed to God, and He didn't let her die. He healed her leg and made it good again. I will ask God to heal yours too, Frau Chusik, if you want me to."

"I will be glad to have you do that," Frau Chusik answered, her voice quivering. She turned her face to hide her emotions.

"Mama says we must believe or He can't help us," Dilek said. Then she closed the door softly and tip-toed across the veranda, thinking that Frau Chusik was a nice lady to visit after all.

Chapter 6

Another Move

Netta's thoughts roamed, flying as swiflty as her knitting needles. Dilek was breathing deeply in sleep. There was no other noise except the click, click of the needles as they wove row upon row onto the garments she and Grandma were knitting to be sold in the city.

Netta drew a deep breath before she began. "I have been wondering if it wouldn't be wise to send Dilek to school, for one term at least."

Netta bent over her knitting again, waiting for Grandma to voice an opinion. Not receiving an answer, Netta continued, "It would mean a little additional sacrificing on our part, but I feel it would be worth it."

Grandma's voice quivered a bit when she spoke. "Couldn't I teach her at home? It would save the cost, at least. I used to teach."

Netta stopped knitting a moment to speak. "To be sure you could, Grandma, but I have thought this thing over and over. I think it would be good for Dilek to mingle more with other children, and, well, to attend a public school."

"Do you think Hans would approve?"

Netta paused to steady her voice. "I think he would, but I have no way to find out. I have to do the best I can. As far as I know, there won't be any teaching to conflict with what we believe. I'm sure no religion will be taught. We can only give it a try, can't we?"

The next afternoon Netta and Dilek were enjoying the hours they could work together in the backyard garden. They had now lived at Luzile for three years, and this was the third summer for a garden. The vegetables from the plot and the milk from Nanny kept the three well fed. At times, they also had enough to share with others.

"Come here, Mama," Dilek called one evening while they were working in the garden. "See if you know what kind of plant this is. It has large prickly leaves, and I don't think it is a weed."

Netta walked to the corner of the garden where Dilek was pulling weeds from an overgrown spot near the fence. "It's a pumpkin or squash plant," Netta exclaimed happily. "Let's pull the weeds around it carefully. Maybe we will have squash to eat before cold weather sets in."

"May I call it my garden?" Dilek asked wistfully.

Netta smiled down into her daughter's eagerly upturned eyes. "Well, since you found the plant which came up voluntarily, it would seem only fair it should be yours. You must keep the weeds out and perhaps water it sometimes."

"Oh, Mama, I will be glad to carry water from the well and take care of it! Is there something else I could plant in my garden? There is some more space in the corner if I clean out all the weeds."

"The pumpkin will grow and spread out, but I think you could put a few turnip seeds there yet."

"Turnips! Oh, good!" Dilek clapped her hands gleefully. "Maybe I can grow a large turnip from my garden like the one Lothar gave us. Remember?" Dilek's face clouded at the thought of the poor children. "I wish Lothar and Tussy were here now. I'm afraid Papa will come too late."

Netta turned as a tear slid down her face. Dilek had such faith. She always talked as if Hans were coming home any day. There were days when Netta wondered if she would ever see her husband again. Then she would cast her fears aside and try hard to trust God as Dilek did.

"If I knew he had found peace, and the Way, it would be easier. God knows. He can help us." These were her thoughts as she picked some beans from the stalks for their supper.

Dilek watched with much anticipation as the vine grew and bloomed. "There are three tiny squashes growing on the vine, Grandma. How soon can we eat them?"

Grandma looked up from her knitting and smiled. "Don't count your chickens before they hatch, dear."

"Chickens?" Dilek frowned inquisitively.

"We must wait and see, Dilek. Sometimes things happen before they grow to maturity."

"But, Grandma, I pull the weeds and take good care of it."

"To be sure, Dilek, you are doing very well. I hope nothing does happen to them. I would like to have some squash to eat soon. I don't want you to count on it too heavily and then for some reason be disappointed."

Netta continued to save. It was not much; yet the bowl in which she kept her savings was getting heavier and was nearly full. She saved for the time when Hans would come. She hoped they could move somewhere else to start a home together. They might even have to leave the country.

She knitted late, and although the earnings were small, it was like Tante Esta said, "It is not much. Yet with careful planning and spending, it does add up."

Netta didn't mind the hard work, knitting late into the night. That they should be fed, and have clothes to wear, and a warm place to stay was all she asked.

A fall chill was in the air when Netta returned from the office and announced that she was to be transferred again.

"Where to?" Grandma asked, weakly laying her knitting aside.

"To Pherd Hoff," Netta answered wearily. "To straighten up another messed-up bookkeeping job."

Grandma picked up her knitting again. "I want to finish this sweater and make the matching cap, at least."

"There isn't time for that, Grandma.

We are to be ready by four in the morning. We must pack at once."

"Mama, Mama, let's not go." Dilek was close to tears. "We want to be here when Papa comes so he can bring Lothar, and so we can eat the squash, and—." Dilek burst into tears.

Netta stroked the head that shook with sobs. "Don't worry. Papa can find us at Pherd Hoff too. We will be closer to him than at Luzile, but further from Lothar. We will ask God to help us in this trial too."

"Mama, may I take the squash over to Frau Chusik? We can't take it along."

Netta thought for a moment. There were poorer people that needed food more than Frau Chusik, but if Dilek had a desire to give her one of her squashes, she would not discourage it.

"Yes, Dilek, but go at once for we have much to do before we leave."

Frau Chusik opened the door at Dilek's knock. "Come in," she said in her former cold tone, but Dilek did not notice.

"I have brought you a squash from my

little garden," she said hurriedly, almost out of breath from running all the way. "We are moving and can't take it along."

"Moving, Dilek? Why?"

"Because they said so at the office. We can't take Nanny either." Dilek choked back the tears that kept coming.

"I'm sorry, Dilek. How soon will you be going?"

"Early in the morning, Mama said. I wish we could stay."

Frau Chusik opened a drawer and pulled out a little brown coat. A pained expression passed over her face as she drew a deep breath. "Let's see if this will fit you." Frau Chusik put the coat around Dilek's shoulders. "A perfect fit, as I thought," she added, as if to herself.

"You may keep this, Dilek." A weak smile replaced the pained frown. "I never thought I would part with this. You see, this was my Mitsy's coat. She was your size when she got killed." Frau Chusik looked out the window with a far-away look in her eyes. "The coat was new. She wore it only once. I want you to have it."

"Oh, it's too nice for me. Really, I—"

Frau Chusik continued to button the coat as though she had not heard. "Where are you moving to?"

"Mama said to Pherd Hoff. I don't know where that is, but nearer to Papa and farther from Lothar. I want Papa to go for Lothar and Tussy, so that—"

"We want many things that cannot be, dear," Frau Chusik said tearfully. "Go now, and thank you for the squash."

Frau Chusik opened the door for Dilek to go, then as if on an impulse, she hugged Dilek hard, shoved her gently out the door, and closed the door.

The gift of the warm coat brought tears to Netta's eyes. "I often wondered if she had sorrows that no one else knew about," she said. "Only the heart knows its sorrows and griefs," she added with feeling.

Dilek was heartbroken to part with Libby. "May we give Nanny to Libby?" she asked Mama. "And dear little Spot. I will never see you again." She wept into his furry skin. "He is purring his farewell," she added, handing him to Libby. Then she turned and fled to her basement apartment.

"Dilek, you must get some rest now," Netta insisted. "The trip will be tiresome and we do not have long to sleep."

"I must say good-bye to Nanny yet, Mama. Then I will rest."

Dilek was soon asleep, but there was no sleep for Grandma or Netta. "We have all we can carry, Grandma. Do not try to pack more. They told me not to take more than we can carry and not more than we need," Netta warned. "If we overdo, they might take some things from us. I would rather leave these things to Frau Molott. She did so much for us."

Grandma was displeased. She had enjoyed the basement home and the knitting that brought them extra income. "It will be a long time before we can find another place like this, I'm afraid. And there will be no knitting to do, and perhaps even more rent to pay."

"We must wait and see. God can help us at Pherd Hoff just as faithfully as He did here in Luzile."

"Here is a bag for you to carry," Netta instructed Dilek. "Someone will meet us at the square, but we must walk that far."

The three walked silently and briskly, well loaded with bundles. The morning air was nippy, and the village was still and dark. A cock crowed in the distance. Dilek kept close to Mama, wishing she had an empty hand to grasp Mama's skirt.

"Your new coat doesn't match the rest of your clothes," Netta remarked softly as they walked under the first street lamp. "But I am thankful you have such a warm one this chilly morning. I hear the wagon coming that will take us to the train depot. We must hurry."

The three climbed onto the wagon, resting their tired arms on the bundles they had carried. Netta soon slept, even though the wagon jolted along rough roads. Grandma dozed too, holding Dilek's head in her lap. It was midmorning before they arrived at the next village, where they were left at the station.

Grandma unwrapped a parcel that contained bread and a bit of cheese made from the goat's milk. "We should eat before the train comes, if we can."

Dilek was hungry and soon swallowed the last of her sandwich. "May I have another, please?"

"Not until noon. If we eat all we have now, we will get too hungry before we arrive in Pherd Hoff," Netta explained.

"I am still hungry, Mama," Dilek said pleasantly, "but not as hungry as when we had no rations. I can wait."

"That's my girl," Netta whispered, smiling at her daughter.

After boarding, they found they had to change trains. "There is no agent at the station where you must wait. Be sure to catch the eastbound train, as it is the only one that goes to Pherd Hoff," the conductor explained. "You will have two hours to wait."

There was only a small, dingy depot, with soot and smoke-covered, broken slat seats. Netta decided to sit on the baggage. "This way we can protect them, I

hope. I don't like the looks of those two."
She nodded toward a suspicious-looking
couple.

However, the man and woman soon left
on the westbound train which pulled in
and stopped only long enough for them to
board.

"We must be alert and ready to board
when our train comes," Netta told Dilek
and Grandma. "Otherwise we may be left
standing here in this station."

"Do you have your pass ready to show?"
asked Grandma.

"I— did he give one to me? The conductor on that train—did he give it to me?"
Netta stammered. She searched through
her purse, but found nothing.

"Surely you have it somewhere, Netta.
Look in your pockets."

Netta's search was fruitless. "We must
find it," she said, her face ashen with fear.

"Let's look under our bags, Mama,"
Dilek suggested, turning hers around.

Netta turned hers to look underneath,
though she knew they could not be there.
She simply did not know where else to

101

look.

"He must not have given them to me," she finally decided. "All I can do is tell the next conductor. But what if he doesn't believe me?"

The station was cold and drafty. Netta stood up. "I must walk to get some circulation going to keep warm. I wish I had some water to wash up a bit."

"I brought a wet cloth along, Netta," Grandma offered.

"Come, Dilek. Let me fix you up first."

Next, Netta slipped off her own head scarf in order to comb back her hair.

"There is a piece of pink paper clipped to your scarf, Mama. Is that the pass?"

Netta looked at her scarf. "Sure enough! How could the conductor have clipped that onto my scarf without my finding out about it?"

The land was more rolling as the travelers neared their destination.

"Look at those hills over there," Dilek pointed out to Netta.

"Those are mountains in the distance. Farther on, this country is very mountainous." The sight of the mountains made her very homesick for her husband. "Hans used to love the mountains," she added sadly.

The village of Pherd Hoff was larger than Luzile. An officer met them at the station. He had not been expecting three, and gave the aged Grandma a disdainful look.

"I am not certain we can use this one," he told Netta, pointing to Grandma. "We asked for the bookkeeper."

"I will need her to stay with my daughter while I work," Netta told him, fear in her voice.

"Your daughter could be placed in a boarding school. Your living quarters will be crowded."

"We will make out," Netta said firmly. "My mother is an experienced teacher and will teach my daughter at home." Suddenly the prospect of sending Dilek to public school seemed less than desirable.

Netta felt like boarding the next train to Luzile, but knew there was little she could do about her circumstances. She

103

was resigned to make the best of it.

"We will see about that later," the officer stormed. "I don't have time to argue with you now. Come."

The officer had been right. The third floor apartment was tiny. Dilek was disappointed that there was no yard to play in.

"No room for a garden or a goat. Not even a cat." Dilek looked about the dark apartment mournfully. "No bed. Nothing."

"Don't talk like that, Dilek. Perhaps we won't live here long. We'll try to make the most of this until we can find a better place."

Grandma and Netta soon had some blankets and bundles ready for beds and the weary ones slept side by side.

"At least the morning sun peeps in this window," Netta said when she awoke. "I must report for work right away. Grandma, you and Dilek see what you can do with this apartment by the time I return."

"I will pray that God will find us

another home where we can have a Nanny again," Dilek said soberly.

"We will do that," Netta said. "If it is His will, we will find one. Maybe He wants us to live here for a while though."

Chapter 7

Dilek Sows

Netta found the work at this office more trying than at Luzile. It was often difficult to get the records to tally up and to find the cause of the errors. Most of all she found the mayor of Pherd Hoff hard to please.

"I sometimes wonder if the mayor really distrusts me or if he just likes to find fault with my work," Netta confided to Grandma one evening after a hard day. "I don't like to cast suspicions, but his honesty seems doubtful at times."

"Perhaps you need to know him better before you judge," Grandma answered with concern. "Surely it would show up on the records if he wasn't."

"What's more, he seems quite familiar with several of the girls at the office, and he is a married man."

"I hope he has not made any advances—?"

"No, Grandma," Netta said with a wry smile. "I'm certain I need not fear that. Really, I think he detests me. I wonder if I would lose my job if—?"

"Do not fear. They sent you here to get things straightened out. I hope you do it honestly, regardless of who may be in the wrong."

"That is what I'm trying to do and—well—I don't want to judge—but trust things will work out."

"I do wish I could find some knitting to do," Grandma said with a sigh. "The rent is higher here than it was at Luzile. With the low wages, it will be tough unless I can help in some way."

"We will trust and watch for an opportunity. But for now, we will have to make the best of it," Netta answered, gazing through the one window of the apartment that gave her a view of the dingy neighboring apartments. But Netta was not seeing the rough concrete walls. Her gaze and thoughts went out, out toward Ultimo. She envisioned a lonely cell that kept Hans within its hard walls. Did they give him enough food to stay alive? Or was he even now being mistreated? She must write him and tell him of their move. They could keep in touch with each other if only by the postage stamp marker to identify where they were staying.

Dilek slapped the book shut that Grandma had given her. Walking over to Mama, she broke into Netta's reverie. "I'm going to find another house to live in!" Dilek vowed emphatically. "I can't see birds or anything else from this window! I have no one to play with!" Her voice choked. She could say no more. Clinging to Mama's full skirt, she sobbed.

Netta gasped, then bit her lip to hide

her own feelings. She felt she dared not give way in Dilek's presence, or weaken the seed of faith that had taken root in her daughter's tender heart.

"We will pray for another home. Perhaps God will see fit to give us one. He can lead us to a place where we can have a goat, if it is His will. The Bible teaches us to be content in every thing. It is not right for us to grumble or complain."

Noticing Dilek's cheeks were getting pale from being shut inside the small apartment most of the time, she added, "I don't want my little girl to lose the roses in her cheeks. Maybe Grandma can take you out for a walk tomorrow. We will have to look for a park so you can play outdoors sometimes."

"I hope Mama finds a park," Dilek chanted, the next morning as she skipped merrily ahead of Grandma. "I want to find one today. I don't want to go back to stay in our dark room."

Dilek turned to see if Grandma was coming. Skipping backwards, she stumbled and fell against the bank of a yard,

"Oh!" She jumped up and brushed the dust from her dress.

"Did you hurt yourself?" a voice called.

Dilek turned to see where the voice came from, just as a slender girl emerged from behind the bushes. "Did you hurt yourself?" she asked again.

"No, thank you," Dilek murmured, blushing as she looked into the dark eyes of the strange girl. "No, I guess I was not looking where I was going," she added, returning the warm smile of the stranger.

"I am Fernella, and I heard you say something about a park. I like to go there too. You are new here, aren't you?" the girl asked, coming closer.

"My name is Dilek. Do you know where there is a park?" Dilek asked hopefully.

"Yes, and I would be glad to go with you sometime, if you want me to."

"Oh, yes." Dilek squealed with delight. "May we go now, Grandma?"

"I don't live here," Fernella explained, pointing to the house behind her. "I just came on an errand and Mama expects me to come right home. I think she would let

111

me go this afternoon, if you'd like."

"What time do you think you could come, and where shall we meet?" Grandma asked, smiling at Dilek's enthusiasm.

"At the village well, if that is convenient."

"Fine. If your mother doesn't object, we will see you at two this afternoon," Grandma promised.

The girls were soon playing together as if they had been well acquainted. They both liked to climb; Fernella showed Dilek the ideal climbing place. An old leaning willow grew at the far corner of the park. Its sweeping, swaying branches beckoned the girls to play.

Fernella taught Dilek to perform athletic stunts. She soon could hang onto the branches by her feet, waving her arms freely. Dilek was nimble and quick to learn. She was not afraid of the heights of the high, flexible limbs.

"Like two monkeys," Grandma described the antics of the two to Netta. "I don't know if I should be glad they found the park or not. Dilek certainly enjoys it, and Fernella is a nice girl. I am glad Dilek has found a friend."

"Let's rest a while," Fernella suggested one day after some strenuous chinning. "Come on up." She motioned to Dilek to take a seat on the branch beside the one on which she was sitting.

"I always meet you at the well, and I don't know where you live," Fernella laughed, sweeping her legs with a thin, leafy willow branch.

"Up that curved street where there are mostly apartment houses. The Narrow, I believe they call it."

"Oh, I know. Where the poor — ah, it really doesn't matter, Dilek," Fernella stammered, afraid she had offended her friend, for she saw a shadow sweep over her countenance. "My papa is rich, I suppose, and we live in a great big house. But, I like to play with you."

"I don't like to live there," Dilek said gravely. "I would rather live out here in this willow tree, but of course, Mama would not let me. I want to live where we can keep a goat and have a cat. I get so

113

lonesome for Spot and Libby." Dilek's face was drawn with sadness and her voice almost broke.

"Who is Spot and who is Libby?"

"Spot is Libby's cat and they are at Luzile. Grandma says if she could find knitting to do like she did at Luzile, we could buy another goat. But we must find another place to live first." Dilek tried to keep back the tears, but they were very near the surface.

"Maybe Mama would let me give you one of our kittens," Fernella said sympathetically.

Dilek brightened for a moment, then broke down and cried. "No, Fernella. Mama said we can't have a kitten before we live in a bigger place than our apartment. Since we don't have a goat, we wouldn't have milk to feed one anyway."

"That's too bad, Dilek. Perhaps later you can have one."

"Yes. We are asking God to help us find another home where we can have a goat. You believe God can help us, don't you, Fernella? Lothar wouldn't believe and he—" Dilek's face looked as if another storm would break.

"Who, Dilek? Who did you say?"

"You mean, who is Lothar? He is still at the Steppes."

"No, Dilek. Who were you going to ask to help you? Your uncle?"

"You mean God? No, Fernella. God lives up there." Dilek pointed up through the leaves where she could see white clouds floating against the blue sky. "He lives up in heaven, but Mama says He is everywhere and can see us and help us."

Fernella looked up through the swaying willow. The breezes gently lifted her flowing hair. Brushing them from her eyes with her hand, she said, "Are you sure? How can anyone live up there in the clouds?"

"Yes, I'm sure, for Mama says so. She said we must trust Him and believe, or it will not please Him. God cares and is able to see us through any bad times."

"I haven't heard anything like that before, Dilek. I will ask my mama about it. Do you want to go to the park again tomorrow?"

"I would like to, but Grandma says she can't come here every day. Listen! Grandma is calling us."

The girls scrambled down from their hideaway and ran to meet her.

"Frau—." Fernella paused; she had not learned Grandma's name.

"Frau Nussbaum," Grandma smiled. "It is easier to call me Grandma as most everyone does."

"That will be nice," Fernella said. "I do not have any grandmother. May Dilek walk with me to the park tomorrow? I could meet her at the well after lessons, then you would not have to bring her if you are busy. I could walk home with her too."

"Thank you, Fernella. I will speak to her mama. We shall see."

Dilek and Grandma convinced Netta that Fernella was a dependable girl that could be trusted to take Dilek safely to the park.

"Since no one older will be going along at times, I expect you to listen to Fernella

116

at the park and on the way," Netta admonished, the next day before leaving for work. "Fernella is the oldest and knows better what to do in case something should happen."

Dilek was pleased to have this privilege and wanted to be sure to live up to her mama's expectations of her.

Later, on the way to the park, Fernella and Dilek returned to their earlier conversation. "I told Mama about God living up there," Fernella pointed upward, "and she says she hasn't heard about God since she was a little girl. She doesn't know if there is still one or not."

Dilek took a deep breath, pondering what Fernella was saying. The two walked on without speaking, both in deep thought.

"Mama also said she thinks if there was still a God, He would not make people suffer so much and let wars come."

"I think that — oh, I do wish Mama were here to explain. She once said that because people do not believe in God and do not love Him, they do many things

117

that displease Him. Sometimes He allows bad people to punish us. She said God loves us and we must love others too, even those that don't treat us very nice."

Dilek moved closer to Fernella and whispered softly, "Don't tell anybody, but it is very hard to love that mean officer that hit me and took our rations away." Fernella listened patiently as Dilek told all about her experience at the canals, her anger, her disobedience and her awful hunger.

"Oh, Fernella, were you ever so hungry you hurt and felt sick down here?" Dilek patted her stomach, then sighed, remembering the hunger pangs. "Only Lothar gave us anything to eat—a big turnip. It was so delicious!"

"I couldn't love that officer either," Fernella stated flatly. She had been taught to love those that love her and to hate those that mistreated her. "In fact, I would want to beat him." She clenched her fists and gritted her teeth.

"No, Fernella. It is a sin to hate or try to get even. We must love those that hate

118

us," Dilek admonished, remembering Mama's instructions. "God loved us when we were bad, and He even sent His Son, Jesus, to die for us, so we can go to heaven to live with Him when we die."

Fernella shook her head. She couldn't understand. "I don't think I want to go to heaven. I want to stay with my mama and papa." Fernella skipped on ahead, hurrying to get to the park.

"They took Papa away, but Mama and I ask God to bring Papa home. He will, too, for we trust Him."

When the girls reached the park, they were soon free from all cares, lost in the fun, romping and playing. Dilek had, however, sown a tiny seed in Fernella's heart that had not been there before.

Netta closed the office door and stepped out into the street with a sigh of relief. She had finished the last accounting record. Everything was filed and accurate. She could lay her finger on all errors and find, in a moment, any record in the office. She had again been an efficient bookkeeper, and her wages were raised slightly. It was not much, but to Netta it was the difference between deprivation and proper nourishment. The strenuous overtime work was leaving its mark on her. She knew her health could not take much more.

Netta breathed deeply of the moist evening air. Would the mayor ever show up at the office again? Hardly. There was evidence that would need explanation if he did. He had made his escape before all the proof was found. His secretary had disappeared with him.

"The evidence is plain," Netta mused to herself. "Both of them are guilty of larceny. The penalty would not be light if they were ever found. I'm certain they know that."

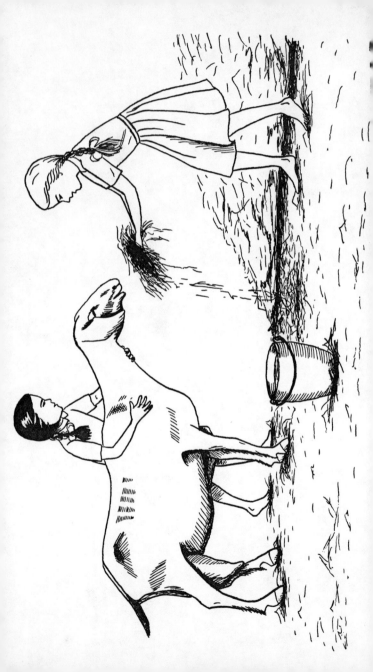

Chapter 8

Answered Prayer

Dilek skipped ahead. She couldn't seem to slow to Grandma's pace when they were headed for the park. "Fernella, Fernella," she hummed. Turning, she waited for Grandma to catch up.

"S-W-A-N. Is that spelled right, Grandma?"

"Yes, dear. I hope you will remember it now." Dilek was anxious to spell *swan* for Fernella for she liked to watch the large white birds float slowly on the water at the park pond.

"I hope I can have some bread for the pretty swans some day," Dilek said, skipping ahead again. "Fernella let me throw her bread to them the last time."

"We must save our rations for ourselves and not waste it," Grandma reminded Dilek again.

Fernella was strangely quiet and absent-minded on the way to the park. "Let's feed the swans first," Dilek chattered. She had looked forward to this afternoon all week. She enjoyed her lessons under Grandma's teaching, but she loved the park.

She loved the birds and their singing, the strutting peacock with his colorful tail trailing him like a bridal veil. But she loved the willow the best of all. Plans and secrets could freely be shared and discussed in its lovely swaying branches. Games of their own inventions could be played without intruders.

To the two girls now entering the park, it was a secret hiding place where lovely music played upon the sweeping strings of the willow when the merry breezes came to play.

"The branches whisper messages to each other," Dilek had said one day. They had giggled at its make-believe mysteries as it sang lullabies to them.

Dilek fed the swans and ducks the few crumbs Fernella had found in one of her pockets. She had forgotten to bring more bread today.

"Don't worry," Dilek comforted, looking at Fernella's sad face. "Maybe we will bring bread the next time. They all look well fed. They probably aren't hungry today anyway."

Fernella turned her head to hide the tears she could not control. Dilek grasped her friend's sleeve. "Are you sick?"

"Please, be quiet, Dilek. I must not speak until we are safe at the willow."

Dilek followed Fernella solemnly. Some great sorrow must surely have come to her friend. She had never seen Fernella cry before.

The girls climbed high into the willow, and Dilek waited until Fernella could compose herself.

"Papa—Papa—he did not come home and—oh, Dilek!" Fernella sobbed, hiding her face in the thick leaves of the willow.

"I am so sorry. Did the police dispatch him?" Dilek tried to comfort her friend by stroking her arm.

"We don't know, Dilek. He never came home, and Mama is afraid he was dispatched to work in the mines. Oh, Dilek, what can we do?"

"They sent my Papa away, too, to work in the mines. Mama cried. She had to work for the government, digging canals and working in the wheat fields. When she hurt her foot, she almost died."

"Mama says we cannot stay in our house without Papa's paycheck. She said maybe she can rent out the rooms for apartments, and live in the basement. Think of that! Dilek, move into the basement!"

Dilek did not think a basement apartment any hardship. She could not think of an answer to comfort Fernella.

"Mama said she cannot afford to keep

me in school either, and she does not want me to be alone if she can find work."

In this manner the two discussed their sorrows and problems in the secrecy of the willow. All play and romping were forgotten.

"Oh, oh! Why didn't I think of it sooner?" Dilek clapped her hands happily, as if all the sorrows in the world had suddenly evaporated. "Mama wants another apartment, if your mama wants to rent one. Do you have a yard for a goat?"

"Why, yes, and we already have a goat."

"God has answered our prayer, Fernella. I have prayed for a home where we can keep a goat and have a garden. Let's run home and ask Mama right away."

"Your mama isn't home yet from work, is she?"

"No. Then, let's pray to God. We will pray for your papa, too, so he will come home again."

"I don't know how to pray, Dilek. You pray and ask God to send Papa home, if He can find him." Fernella was again in tears.

"God knows, Fernella. He knows where your papa is. Come, let's pray under the willow. See? You get down on your knees," Dilek said, demonstrating. "Then, close your eyes tight; we must not see God."

Fernella looked about to make sure no one was looking before she knelt beside Dilek.

Dilek began to pray. "Dear God, please take care of my papa and bring him home. Please take care of Fernella's papa too, and let us have a room at her home and a goat. Amen."

Fernella repeated part of the prayer, then opened her eyes, looking quickly behind herself, as if Papa would appear immediately. "I'm scared, Dilek. Are you sure God hears and cares?" Fernella whispered shakily.

"Of course He does, Fernella. We must trust God to do it, Mama said." Dilek spoke firmly, but her face was troubled and sad. A tear slid down her cheek.

"You asked God only to send home your papa, Dilek. Why?"

"I know it was bad, Fernella, but if your papa comes home, we will not be able to live in your apartment." Dilek covered her face with her hands and shook with sobs.

The heavy decision between living in a more favorable home and having God bring Fernella's papa home battled within her heart for a long moment. Her sobs subdued. Smiling through her tears, she cheerfully said, "I will pray again."

Dropping to her knees, she prayed earnestly, "Please bring Fernella's papa home. Forgive me for being selfish. And please, dear God, find a home for us with a garden and a goat."

Having prayed, Dilek's guilty heart was at peace. She got up from her knees with trust and peace.

"Come in. I am Frau Rutini." The lady who answered their knock welcomed Netta and Dilek inside. "I have been expecting you. Since it was children's plans, I wasn't certain whether you'd come." Frau Rutini smiled, offering her hand. "I will call Fernella. She will be glad to have

Dilek."

Netta was glad to have a few moments alone when Frau Rutini excused herself to call Fernella. A pattern was shaping in her thoughts. Rutini, the mayor's name. Fernella's papa was gone. Perhaps she should not inquire about an apartment. Looking about the well-furnished room, she decided the Rutinis were some of the wealthier citizens of Pherd Hoff.

Frau Rutini returned, breaking into Netta's reverie. "You girls may go outside to look at the goat and kittens," Frau Rutini smiled. Turning to Netta she added, "I am happy to have your daughter as Fernella's friend. She has told me of their good times at the park."

Encouraged by Frau Rutini's friendliness, Netta asked, "Are you Mayor Rutini's wife?"

"I am, and you are the new bookkeeper. Dilek told Fernella that your husband was dispatched too. It is hard." Frau Rutini supressed a sob and wiped the tears that kept pushing themselves to the surface.

Netta arose and went to embrace Frau Rutini. "I know. It is too heavy to bear alone. But there is One who wants to help us bear our burdens and sorrows. I have found much strength and comfort in His promises."

"I wish I had such faith, Frau Reimer. Fernella tried to tell me what Dilek said, but I don't know how to get hold of myself. We are now poor, and unless I rent the house and find work, I don't know what will become of us."

"That reminds me of why we came. Dilek thought it might be possible to rent an apartment. She will give me no rest until we find out."

"I would be glad to rent out a basement apartment which would be less expensive. If I can rent the upper apartments, I plan to move into the basement too. Come and see if you like what I have in mind."

Netta found there were two basement apartments. She was delighted with the one Frau Rutini had planned for them. There was a small kitchen that both could use. Then there was a small bedroom for

Grandma. They would have ample space in the one other room for both living quarters and another bedroom.

"Now, come and see the courtyard. I would like to keep this backyard with the basement apartments. We could keep the goat for milk and have a garden."

"Dilek says Grandma could teach me too," Fernella whispered joyfully. Dilek shared her plans to feed and water the goat.

Frau Rutini smiled at their enthusiasm. "It seems as if the girls were doing the planning and we the following. But Fernella, we must not impose on Grandma until we can ask her. Perhaps she will not want another pupil."

"I'm certain Grandma would be glad to teach Fernella too. It would be more interesting for Dilek to have another pupil in school. The bit of added work will not overload Grandma. As for the apartment, it's wonderful, in more ways than one."

Chapter 9

Reunited

Netta arranged a short period of worship and Sunday school on Sunday mornings, which consisted mostly of singing hymns that Netta remembered. She had a gifted voice and had sung in the girls' choir at Sunday school. She also taught Dilek some of the Bible verses she could recall. How she longed for more material, especially a Bible, but it seemed none could be found.

Although these worship services were

quite primitive, they strengthened their faith and brought a deeper desire to learn more, to serve God in truth. Dilek grew in the knowledge of the Word, in its simplicity. Worshiping together also was a means of reviving their spirits that waned by the end of the week.

"Let's ask Fernella to Sunday school," Dilek pleaded the first Sunday morning they lived in the Rutini's apartment. "It is such fun to have her in school, and it would be nicer to have another girl in Sunday school too. Please, Mama!"

"Maybe we should not bother them this time, dear. They may be accustomed to sleeping longer on Sunday mornings since there is no church to go to. Perhaps later we can ask them."

Netta led in singing and Grandma and Dilek blended their voices with hers.

"Fear not, I am with thee,
Oh, be not dismayed;
For I am thy God,
I will still give thee aid.
I'll strengthen thee,
Help thee, and cause thee to stand. . . ."

136

Netta could not recall the last line of the song so they finished by humming, Dilek keeping time with her hands and feet.

The three sang the last verse with full volume, for this was their favorite and brought them courage to face the future.

"The soul that on Jesus hath leaned for repose,
I will not, I will not desert to his foes;
That soul though all hell should endeavor to shake,
I'll never, no never, no never forsake."

"Let's sing 'Jesus Loves Me,' " Dilek said. She could lead that one. It was so full of Jesus' love for her that she never grew tired of hearing it.

After the first verse, there was a gentle knock on the door. Netta went to see who their early visitor might be. It was Frau Rutini and Fernella.

"Come in, come in," Netta invited. "I hope we didn't disturb you, but we are happy to have you join our worship."

"We would like to, if we are not intruding. We could no longer resist the temptation to come, just to hear the beautiful singing."

"I do not remember many songs. Perhaps you can help us revive our memories."

"I wish I could. It has been so long since I heard such singing. We will just listen. Perhaps we can learn."

Netta led in the hymn "What a Friend We Have in Jesus." Frau Rutini soon joined in humming the tune with them, then helped with the words. The serenity of the tune and the comfort of the words brought tears to her eyes.

"Oh, Frau Reimer, we have missed so much these past years," Frau Rutini wept after the song ended. "Had we been more concerned about spiritual things, it might be different for us now. We are reaping what we have sowed, no doubt."

"I know how you feel, Frau Rutini. We have suffered much for our sins and neglect. I am seeking to learn more of the truth. God has been merciful, and has given me more light and greater joy than I thought possible in our trials, since I seek Him earnestly.

"I will quote a few verses I learned in Sunday school years ago. I know the Bible never changes, for it is God's Word. Maybe the girls can learn one of them," Netta suggested. "I think the Bible verses you learn when you are young can be priceless later on. You remember them more easily than when you memorize them later in life."

"Blessed are the merciful, for they shall obtain mercy."

"Blessed are the pure in heart, for they shall see God."

"Love thy neighbour as thyself."

Netta quoted each verse clearly. "We will learn the first Bible verse today, and see if the girls can memorize the other two by next Sunday morning."

"What does the Bible mean by 'pure in heart'?" Frau Rutini asked.

"It is found in the part of the Bible that we call the Beatitudes. Our hearts should be pure, then I think our thoughts and motives will be pure too. I know we need the cleansing of the Holy Spirit. We need to have our sins washed in the blood of Jesus. This is perhaps hard to understand, for I need to know more myself. I have so much to learn. I pray that sometime we again may have a Bible and a minister to explain these things.

"Truthfully, circumstances look dark to us at times, but we must learn to trust God and do what we know is right until we can learn more." Netta stopped short to catch her breath, somewhat abashed at the sermonette. It was the first time that anyone other than the family had been present at their worship hour.

"Let's close our eyes and pray to God for understanding and for safekeeping," Netta said softly. "Then we will sing another song."

"I hope we may come again next Sunday." Frau Rutini said with feeling before she left. "It has meant much to me. And Fernella needs to have such teachings as well. Do you think some might oppose a worship meeting if it was made known?"

"I think so, Frau Rutini. It would be best not to mention it because it might conflict with government rules, if they became aware of what we are trying to teach our children."

Dilek and Fernella were apt pupils under Grandma's gentle training. Not only did they grow in knowledge and good manners, but also in their understanding of God. Their work in the garden and barn, besides a regular routine at the park, kept them physically fit, too. Grandma arranged wisely to let them have time off for play, as well as for work.

"I will bring hay for Nanny," Dilek said to Fernella. It was the fall of the year and the days were beginning to shorten.

"All right," Fernella nodded in agreement. "I will bring the grain so she can eat while I milk her."

Dilek sprang to the top of the hay stack. She dug out an armful of hay and turned to slide down again. Suddenly she stopped, sitting at the top, her feet dangling. Her gaze was fixed on the man that had just entered the yard by slipping through a gap in the hedge.

Dilek blinked as if she thought the

man might disappear. A fear gripped her heart. She noticed he did not wear the gray officer's uniform. Who could it be?

Now the man noticed Dilek on the hay stack and came staggering, almost stumbling in her direction. How thin and poor he looked. Dilek's heart was touched at his appearance. She had not forgotten her own hunger of years ago.

"Is—are you—?" the man spoke with effort.

"Papa! Papa!" Dilek cried in an undertone. Even in her excitement, she had not forgotten to keep quiet, so as not to arouse suspicion. Her hay was forgotten. She slid down into her Papa's arms.

"Is it really you? Dilek! My darling child!"

Dilek clung to her papa, with arms around his neck, wetting his face with her tears. "You dear, poor Papa. Come. Mama will give you something to eat." She sobbed again.

"There, there, Honey. It is all right," he said soothingly.

Dilek drew him toward the house. The

next moment Netta and Hans were in each other's arms.

Mother and daughter almost carried Papa inside, for he was so weak he nearly collapsed before he reached the door.

Netta quickly got hot soup ready and spooned some of the broth into her husband's starved lips. "Lie right here until you are revived a bit. Oh, Hans, it's been so long—." She wept over his wretched appearance. She, too, had experienced starvation, and remembered what sort of suffering her husband must have gone through.

"Netta, this is the best soup I've ever tasted," Hans said a bit later, sitting up. "I think I can handle a bowlful now."

Netta and Dilek did not eat. Papa could have all the soup. They enjoyed seeing Papa satisfy his hunger and did not mind missing their supper.

"You must just eat and sleep until you have regained your strength," Netta cautioned. "We have much to tell you, but not tonight. It can all wait until you are rested."

"I have some good news," Papa said one evening, a week later having regained some of his strength. "The Lord has been good to spare me when many of my companions died from starvation and hard labor at the mines. Even then, a group of believers had many blessings and added strength and joy beyond anything we could have hoped for. One kind old brother who loved the Lord was Herr Yuhimson. He had memorized much of the Bible. At night when we all gathered around the small stove to get all its warmth, he would teach us about God and the saving power of His Son, Jesus, who came into the world to redeem lost mankind.

"This brother also prayed, while we crowded around the stove, that barely kept us from freezing when the temperature dropped to 50 below. He invited us to accept God's free gift of salvation. I was one of the four that found the Lord one night."

"I had been praying that some one might bring you to the Lord," Netta said

144

softly. "I cannot thank Him enough for keeping you safe."

"I did not know how to pray, and when I got to prison, my first cell was so small, there was only the usual narrow bunk, and a small wood stove. I felt that I was being watched, even when the door was closed, but I could not go to sleep without praying to God, and brother Yuhimson was not there to pray for me. I dropped on my knees behind the stove and said the Lord's Prayer. I thought the Lord knew my needs better than I did, and He would understand."

Netta pressed Hans' hand, while tears, of feeling too deep for words, coursed down her cheeks.

"I went to bed that night with peace in my heart, sleeping as soundly as if no death sentence hung over me." Hans continued with an assuring smile.

"The Bible verses I learned from this dear brother sustained me in my lonely prison cell. They gave me hope and courage, especially when I realized my sentence meant death. But the day of my execution never came. God knew I was guiltless, as I had told the officers. I also had told them I was ready to die. Yet I longed to have a chance to see you and Dilek once more. Yes, the Lord has indeed been merciful to me.

"They shifted me from one prison to the next. Always I thought my time had come. At the last prison there was another, a young man, who was also a guiltless prisoner. I got to know him quite well. When this boy's papa came to visit, he would talk with me too."

Hans paused, tired from his long speech.

"I had the privilege of several private converstions with this man. I told him we came from the former Mennonite homes and were seeking to know more of the truth. I hoped we could find some believers to fellowship with, as a church."

"Oh, Hans, were you not afraid someone might report you? Then they would have carried out the sentence." Netta spoke fearfully.

"No, I was not afraid. I was willing to

146

die, not being guilty of any offense. This dear brother told me we could find brethren and a church at Nustali, about four hundred miles northeast from here."

"How can we go, Hans?" Netta questioned with interest. "We have saved up a little, but not much."

"We want to go as soon as we can get enough funds. Part of the way we must walk, to throw off any suspicion."

"I hate to leave Frau Rutini and Fernella. They, too, are seeking for more understanding. Fernella is growing in the faith already, as is her mother, I believe. If we leave them, I fear—"

"Perhaps they would be interested in moving with us to."

Dilek realized this move would take them further away from the Steppes where they had left Lothar and Tussy. She begged Papa to go and get them first.

"Lothar wanted me to stay to teach him about God, Papa. I can't forget them. He helped us when we had no rations—" Dilek could not finish because of the lump that choked her throat. She threw her

147

arms around Papa's neck and wept.

"Don't fret, Sweetheart," Papa said soothingly. "We must make plans and see what we can do. In the meantime, I hope to get a few small jobs to help with our needs."

Hans stroked the soft waves of his daughter's hair affectionately. "You must try to be good, Dilek. Learn your lessons quickly so Grandma has more time to knit. The more you are willing to cooperate, the sooner we can move." Papa sounded so hopeful that the sunny smile returned to Dilek's face. She promised to do her best.

Chapter 10

In Search of Fellowship

Hans found some paint jobs. Most of them were not near home; often he had to find other lodging. When he did come home, he came at dusk or after dark. No one in the village except the Rutinis knew that Netta Reimer's husband had been released from prison and had come home.

Slowly but surely, the goal they strived for became reality. Frau Rutini also made plans to join the Reimers. She sold what furniture she could without arousing suspicion. Much planning and counseling took place during the night. They were thankful for their dark basement apartments, an added measure of secrecy.

"I think it would be safest to send you three ladies alone with the children, while I go to see about Lothar and Tussy. We would need to go in different directions, after traveling by foot one night. Even then, it would be best if you would travel as two separate parties," Hans explained. "It would cause less reason for suspicion. The fact that I am released from prison, does not mean they can't pick me up again. My sentence was to have been for at least five more years, unless the death sentence was carried out sooner."

Again the Reimers left all. They took only their clothes, as though they were going on a week's vacation.

Hans and Netta didn't sleep. They rehearsed their plans that night. They would leave at midnight and walk as a group to Westvisten in time to catch the train. "It may be best to go that way, even if it's not the most direct route. Your train will then make connections for the big city. From there you can buy a ticket for Nusstali. Don't forget the name I put on paper. Ask for him at the station; he will help you. The God who brought us together again is able to help us now. Keep courage, trust in God, and may He direct you and keep you safe."

These were comforting words for Netta. This time she could depend on Hans to make the plans. She needed only to follow.

"We need to talk now, for once we are outside, we should not say much," Hans told the solemn group that was ready to start on their journey. "One mistake may mean more partings and sorrow. We must think wisely and follow instructions before we make a move. We will now commit our all to God, who is able to do that which is impossible." After they all bowed their heads, Hans prayed softly, and the group filed silently out into the night.

The girls carried only small packages in which were packed their daily provisions. Hans, Netta, Grandma, and Frau Rutini each carried a piece of luggage. They were traveling light to make the stretch on foot more easy and fast. Netta had no regrets about what she had to leave behind this time. The eyes of all were fixed on the future. No earthly gain could compare to the value of being together, and of having a church where they could worship God.

Dilek gripped Papa's hand as they hurried across some rough farm fields. They headed south, though their destination lay east and north.

"From now on, we are different parties," Hans reminded them for the last time, as they emerged from a wooded area near the highway that led to the town where the women and children would board the train.

Dilek pressed Papa's hand before she released her hold. There was no commotion. There were no words, though fear clutched at her heart. This might be a final parting. Yet joy filled her heart to think that Papa was going, to try to bring Lothar and Tussy.

Netta turned at the corner. They were now on the busy street which led to the depot. She did not glance to see which way Hans went, but was aware that he was no longer with them.

An officer in gray uniform passed by scrutinizing them. "He found nothing amiss," thought Netta, "for he kept on walking."

The throng in the street was pressing; most of the people were going in the direction of the depot.

"I'm sorry," a man said as he brushed hurridly by, whipping Dilek's package from her grasp, and sending it scooting down the street. An old lady stumbled on it and frowned.

The man wove through the crowd of moving feet and brought back the parcel. "I'm sorry," he said again, pressing the parcel and a piece of money into Dilek's hand. Then he was gone.

Dilek was so frightened by the sudden

incident that she clung to Netta's hand. She even forgot to say *Thank you* to the kind gentleman.

Netta arranged the parcel so it would be more convenient for Dilek to carry. "Don't act frightened, dear," she whispered. "And don't forget your manners."

When Netta got to the station, she realized why the crowd had hurried. The train to the big city was almost due.

Netta, Grandma, and Dilek waited their turn at the end of the line before the ticket agent. Dilek noticed without turning her head that Fernella and her mother were waiting in the other line. In their scramble, they had lost sight of each other.

"Run!" the ticket agent said as he handed Netta the tickets.

Netta half dragged Dilek down the narrow passage and through the gate. They ran past coach after coach, and came, gasping for breath, to the one that was loading.

The conductor did not take time to inspect their tickets before lifting and pushing Grandma up the steps ahead of him. Grabbing Dilek, he pitched her after Grandma. Netta grabbed the hand rail just as the train began to move forward slowly.

"A close call," the conductor muttered. "People always seem to wait until the last minute."

Netta dropped into an empty seat, exhausted. The train was so crowded she had to hold Dilek on her lap. "Did Frau Rutini and Fernella get on?" Netta wondered. She could see ahead through most of the coach, but could not see anyone that resembled their friends.

"Father," she prayed silently, "keep them in Your hands, and keep us this day. Be with Hans and hasten his mission, if not against Your will."

"Can we eat now?" Dilek pulled on Mama's sleeve. "I am so hungry."

Netta nodded, unwrapping Dilek's parcel. "I am hungry too."

Carefully they divided the food. They ate sparingly. The small supply must last for another day at least, or until they reached their destination. If they failed to make connections, they would have to do without food for the last stretch of their journey.

Netta, Grandma and Dilek were ushered with the throng into the enormous city depot. "A sea of people," murmured Netta. It made her dizzy.

"We must stick together," Netta warned Dilek and Grandma, "or we will lose each other."

Netta searched for the information center and learned they had a two hours' wait before their train was due. She looked for the ladies' room, where they found seats to rest.

Netta watched closely as the other women and children came and went. Still she did not see Frau Rutini and Fernella. Her heart reached out in concern. "Father," she prayed again, "they are seeking You in sincerity. If they lose out now, where will they be able to learn more? Keep them, O God."

Having cast her burden on the One who knows and cares and helps, Netta rested

158

her head against the cushioned couch and fell asleep. Dilek also slept, with head cradled in her mama's lap. Grandma alone kept watch over their belongings.

A woman officer made her rounds to check the lounge room. Stopping to question Grandma, she kept an eye on Netta and the sleeping child.

"What station did you come from?" she asked, authority marking each word.

Grandma fumbled nervously for the tickets. Finally she wakened Netta. As in a nightmare, Netta searched for the tickets and handed them over. The officer took them and left the room, mumbling, "I must get these checked."

Netta frowned. Would the officer bring them back in time? "It was only a short nap," she told Grandma, "but it helped my headache. It's nearly gone."

Netta watched the clock. Thirty minutes passed and the officer had not yet returned. In another thirty minutes, the train was due to depart. It was time to make preparations to board, yet they dared not leave the place where they were waiting.

They waited, silently, painfully. Each minute seemed to tick faster; waiting became torture. Netta hoped she need not rush as they had rushed at the other station. Yet she knew impatience would not help. It might only cause suspicion.

The officer returned saying all was in order. Netta gathered their belongings and entered the long depot still swarming with travelers. She passed a stately, stern-looking officer who gave them a quick inspection, but let them pass. The train was five minutes late. They boarded it in plenty of time.

Walking through the coach, Netta saw that Frau Rutini and Fernella were already seated. She gave thanks to God and found seats. There was room for all of them this time.

Chapter 11

Lothar Returns

Netta, Grandma, and Frau Rutini, Dilek and Fernella were happily reunited when they arrived at Nusstali. Christian friends made them welcome in their homes while they awaited the arrival of Hans.

Dilek visited the small orchard on the knoll twice a day to pray for Papa and Lothar. She would climb a gnarled old apple tree and look out in the direction from which she hoped to see Papa come.

"I think it would be well for Dilek and Fernella to start school with the other children here," Netta said one morning. "Time would pass more quickly, and the children would not get so far behind in their studies."

Frau Rutini agreed. "The house would not be as crowded during school hours, at least. The children will enjoy this school, I'm sure."

Dilek was reluctant to start to school before Papa arrived, but she soon made new friends, and was happily occupied.

"Did Papa come today?" was the first question she always asked as soon as she arrived home from school. Her eyes always searched for an added person in their group.

Frau Rutini found work in a factory and rented an apartment. Fernella and Dilek were parted now, except in school. Netta waited to counsel with Hans before accepting work.

Dilek's joy was complete when Papa and Lothar walked in, one morning almost a month after they and Frau

Rutini had arrived.

Dilek was soon wrapped in her father's arms. "Papa, Papa," was all she could say, but her sparkling eyes asked volumes.

"Tussy died," Hans whispered, close to her ears.

Dilek shook hands with Lothar. How thin and tall he was. "I'm so happy that you came," Dilek exclaimed sincerely.

Lothar withdrew his hand shyly from Dilek's firm grip, acknowledging her welcome with a slight nod. But his face remained rigid and sad.

"It is time to go to school now," Dilek said, giving Papa a kiss. "Bye now, see you tonight," Dilek waved. "We can talk then," she whispered in an undertone to Lothar.

Dilek could not keep her thoughts on her lessons that day. She could hardly wait to speak alone with Lothar and learn what had caused the fear and sadness that were written on his face.

Dilek coaxed Lothar to her private haven in the orchard. She realized they would have to be alone if she were to be able to drag him out of his stiff shell.

"Tell me about Tussy," Dilek asked, when at last they were alone.

"After Mama died, Tussy just mourned, silently. She no longer cared; often she didn't eat. Her eyes would stare when I talked; she saw and heard no one. One morning she was gone. Thinking she might have gone to gather dried grass, I went to bring water from the canals, and—" Lothar turned his face and breathed deeply.

"Oh, Dilek. It was awful! She lay in the water, drowned."

"Lothar, I'm so sorry," Dilek reached out to touch Lothar's arm in sympathy. "Did you stay alone?"

Lothar supressed another sob, but Dilek heard. Tears sprang to her eyes. How he had grown, and yet he was so thin. They must give him more food. Tight lines of grief and loneliness deepened on his forehead.

Lothar picked up a twig and snapped it in two. "Yes, I stayed alone when I was at the tent, but I started to roam, and I know it was wrong according to your God, but I wanted to get revenge. They had killed Mama by making her work too hard and by not supplying enough food. I started to steal," Lothar whispered fiercely, pitching the twigs away with force.

Dilek was afraid of the flashing eyes and of the hate she saw in them. "Oh, Lothar, don't," she pled, catching hold of his shirt sleeve. "It is sin to hate."

Lothar jerked free and jumped up from the stump where he had been sitting. His fists clenched, he hissed through gritted teeth, "I'll get even yet. I'll get revenge, if I have to die getting it."

"No, no! Oh, Lothar, you must learn to love! Love is much stronger than hate. Please, Lothar, you will stay with us," Dilek stated rather than asked, voice quivering with emotion.

Lothar slumped down again on the stump. The fire had gone from his eyes. Dilek was the first person to whom he had unburdened his heart. He covered his face with both hands, ashamed of his tears and of his frankness. "Your papa

167

was so kind to come for me. I was desperate, ready to fight anyone I met."

"I could not think of moving still further away without sending Papa to bring you. I prayed often, Lothar, that God would keep you until Papa came home. I want you to learn more about God now that we have a church to go to."

Hans found a tiny cottage at the edge of the village. They would be crowded, but all had learned to live with worse conditions than those. Dilek and Grandma shared one room while Lothar slept on a pallet in the main quarters that also served as kitchen and living room.

Frau Rutini's apartment was not near to the Reimer's, much to Fernella and Dilek's disappointment.

"You will see each other in school," Netta comforted the girls.

Hans found some odd jobs for Lothar. Sometimes Lothar went with him to learn to paint. He was restless and rather shy in the home of the Reimers. Although they made every effort to make him feel welcome, he felt he was interfering

168

with the family's privacy.

Only when he was alone with Dilek would he pour out his uncertainties. "I'm always the odd number, Dilek. I think I should look for another home."

Dilek was hurt. "How can you say that? You should be happy to have a home now. We count you as one of us. Truly, Lothar, we all want you to stay."

"You are all so kind, Dilek," was all that Lothar managed to say, but Dilek did not like the far away, forlorn look in his eyes.

Hans was appointed janitor and door-keeper at the church. He was willing and eager to work for the church, no matter how humble the work might be. The Reimers hungered to learn the truths of the Bible. They sank in the simple sermons that Brother Ulrich preached. Though he lived in a distant village and could not be present every Sunday, the small group at Nusstali met every Sunday for Scripture reading and singing. They spent much time in prayer for the safety of Brother Ulrich and for the

169

enlightenment of the congregation to understand God's will and His gift of salvation through faith in His Son Jesus. All were seeking to find that which had been lost during previous years.

"You know that the government has forbidden to allow our children into the church?" a well-meaning brother told Hans the first Sunday morning as he took his place at the door.

"We do well to listen to the Word of God instead of the government in this matter," Hans answered with feeling and concern for the younger generation. "We dare not turn any away."

Though realizing anew that he could be arrested and sent back to prison or to the mines, Hans thought it worth the risk to let the children hear the Word of God. The small congregation grew.

Dilek grew quickly in the knowledge of the Bible. She learned Bible verses, for they had no Bible of their own. In fact, she could often quote more verses than her elders.

"I must learn more so I can teach

Lothar," she told her mama one day. "I wish he would try harder to learn them."

"Don't become weary in well doing, Daughter," Netta advised kindly. "I think your efforts are taking a deeper root in Lothar's heart than you think. You will never regret what you learn now. I only wish I could learn as easily as you."

Dilek enjoyed going to fetch water at the village well. She went early enough to bring some before she went to school. Growing strong and energetic, she enjoyed these early morning walks immensely. She would sing softly each new hymn she was learning. It seemed as if she could talk to God through song. She felt His presence very near.

"Who else but God could have taught the birds when and where to nest? Why did the robin build his nest in a tree, while the swallow daubs mud nests to the rafters of the old mill? Who told the violets by the path that it was springtime again? Who gave them that rich purple color? Who makes everything? Only God could! What a dear, wise, wonderful God!"

She neared the mill and stopped to look at the stream where some ducks were swimming lazily, diving now and then into the water, then bobbing their heads up with mud squirting from their wide bills.

Dilek wished the mill would still be operating. She often tried to visualize the friendly miller who had ground the wheat into meal and flour. Were he there now, he would come to the door to wave or speak, his clothes powdered dusty and white.

Dilek did not linger long. Her thoughts went to the little boy living in the next house. Would he be awake so early this morning? Would he try to throw pebbles into her pail of water?

"What a dear, naughty little boy," she mused. She missed him if he did not come out or wave from his window.

Dilek hurried to the well, breathing deeply as she lengthened her strides. Vibrant and glowing, she thought how good it was to be alive and to be among friends. Her thoughts turned to Lothar.

"Why doesn't he believe in God?" Dilek wondered.

After filling her pail and drinking a cup of the fresh cool water, she retraced her steps. "Good morning, Roscoe," Dilek greeted the little boy in the yard. "It's good to see you out so bright and early this morning," she added pleasantly, hoping he would not try any of his tricks. She noticed his little fist was tightened around something.

"I have something for you," she called cheerily. "See?" Dilek held out her hand with a piece of sugared bun in it. Roscoe hid his fist behind his back, reaching through the pickets for the sweet bun with his other hand.

"You will be good now, won't you?" Dilek coaxed, patting his arm. Would she dare tell him a Bible story? "I will tell you a story about a little boy who gave his lunch to Jesus so that many people who were hungry could eat. Yes, this is a true story. He had only five loaves of bread and two fish in his lunch, but Jesus thanked God for it, and then there was plenty to

173

feed—"

Roscoe had been interested as long as the bun lasted. Then, quick as a flash, he threw his fistful of pebbles and dirt into Dilek's pail of water, then fled behind the house.

The first time this happened, Dilek felt like running after the bad little boy to teach him a lesson. Now her newly-found Bible truths made her only love him more. She longed to teach him to be kind and thoughtful. So, she thought, I must not fuss at him.

"After all, Jesus did not scold or hit back. I must learn to be more like Him," she thought aloud, as she went back to the well for another bucket of clean water.

Dilek had an impulse to walk home by another street. Then she decided otherwise. She would simply guard her pail more carefully this time. *I have no time to waste now, but I do want to be friendly to Roscoe so that one day I may win him. He is so dear.*

Roscoe was waiting again, fist filled. Dilek turned her back to catch the pebbles this time; then hurried on, smiling and waving to the little boy who was so full of pranks.

"What was that?" Dilek stopped long enough to listen when she passed the old mill. "Kittens, I do believe!"

Dilek hurried on. "Tonight, maybe Lothar will come with me to see if we can find them. I need to talk with him privately again, anyway."

"Are you sure you heard kittens?" Lothar asked as they waded through the tall weeds along the edge of the stream, keeping close to the side of the mill.

"I'm almost certain. The sounds came from this direction."

"Here are some loose boards. I think I could easily get inside."

"Do you think we should?"

"No one is ever around here. We are not here to do harm."

The boards bent easily. "Be careful. Lothar, the board floor might be rotten," Dilek gasped as the boards creaked beneath their weight.

"They seem solid enough. It's a bit

spooky in here."

"I don't believe in spooks. Ee-ow! Lothar, what was that?"

"Ho, ho! Don't believe in spooks, huh? But you just screamed at a poor little mouse running away from you across the floor."

"Listen, Lothar! Stop laughing. I hear the kittens again."

"They must be back against the wall we just came through."

"There is a hole in the floor here. I think they are down here somewhere." Dilek knelt and pried at the loose board.

"You're wrong, Dilek," Lothar whispered. "I feel something warm and wiggly behind this brace. See? It is stuffed with rags and makes an ideal place for a cat's nest."

"I can barely touch them, Lothar. Can't you get them out? I'd like to see them."

"Hold out your arms. I'll try to get them for you."

Lothar reached down and brought out a furry kitten. Dilek squealed with delight as she held the soft ball of warmth in her arms. "Any more, Lothar?"

"Here are two more. Three in all."

"One is white, pure white. Oh, I wish we could take him home." Dilek rubbed her cheek against the fuzzy little creature. "But I know he is too young to leave his mother yet."

"Here comes the mother cat now, Dilek. She may not like for us to handle her babies."

Dilek stroked the cat. She seemed tame and friendly enough. "Lothar, let's not put them back into that hole. Can you dig out the rags? We can make a nest here in this wooden box now that the mama cat has seen where her babies are."

Lothar reached again into the nest and pulled out a rag. "Looks like an old miller's coat." Lothar shook out the musty, ragged garment. "Good enough for a cat's nest, I suppose."

"Put it in the box. Then the mama can nurse them. They are hungry. Look how they nuzzle at my finger. How cute they are!"

Dilek tried to smooth the soiled coat

177

into a soft nest. Her hand touched a flat, hard object. "There is something in this pocket. Come, Lothar, see what it is."

Lothar fumbled for the pocket. He pulled out a small book. "Who could have left this, Dilek?"

"The miller, of course. You said it was a miller's coat." Dilek settled the kittens into their new nest. "Let me see that."

"It's a Bible, I'm quite sure," Dilek gasped. "The miller hid it, and God let us find it. Oh, Lothar, I wish I could read it."

"It will do no good if no one can read it, Dilek. Let's put it back into the hiding place."

"No, no, Lothar. I must show Papa first. Maybe he can read it."

"I would rather put it back," insisted Lothar stubbornly. "I hear enough from the Bible as it is."

Dilek took the Book from Lothar's hand and quickly slipped it into her skirt pocket. "It may not be a Bible, Lothar, but I do want Papa to see it."

"Come then. We must go," Lothar answered roughly, plainly showing his displeasure.

"Lothar," Dilek began as soon as they were outside the mill. "Can't you see the hand of God everywhere? Look at the swallows nesting in the eaves. They are returning for the night. Who told them to use mud for their nests and who taught the young ones to dart about so quickly? Watch them catching insects in the air. Look at the flowers coming out in the warm summer sun. Who but God could make all the beautiful things that grow in spring?"

"Nature is going on as it always did, Dilek. I still cannot believe a good God would let so many bad things happen to one person." Lothar answered sadly, but Dilek noticed his anger was subdued.

"I hope this is a Bible and that Papa can read it. Knowing that it is God's written message to us, we must believe. Lothar, I will not cease to pray that God will give you light to see and believe. And I'll pray that someday you will receive the Lord Jesus into your heart."

"Thank you, Dilek." Lothar's voice was

husky as he added, "I am not worth all the effort you put on me." He touched her arm.

"I can only pray, Lothar. I can try to teach you about God, but I can't make Jesus come into your heart. You must do that yourself. No one can invite Him into your heart but you."

"Maybe someday I will understand more, Dilek. Have you invited Him into— your heart?" Lothar stammered, wanting to know, yet hesitating to ask such a personal question.

"I have invited Him in, Lothar. He came and made me new." Dilek shed tears of happiness. "Oh, Lothar, it is so wonderful to have Him! He gives such joy when He cleanses from all our sins, Lothar, all sins. Not just part of them, but all!"

The two walked a short distance in silence, each in thought.

"And Lothar, I want to say this yet. I have not told anyone, not even Papa or Mama. I had to make this decision myself, too. I want to be baptized. The Bible says that whoever believes in his heart and confesses with his mouth the Lord Jesus, the same shall be saved. It also says that if we believe, we should be baptized."

"When, Dilek?"

"I don't know when. As soon as there is an opportunity. When a minister comes again. And, Lothar, I had hoped you would want to be baptized at the same time. But first you must trust in God and believe on His Son Jesus."

"No, Dilek. I am not as good as you. God would not have me."

Dilek turned to face Lothar. "No one is good, Lothar. God says if we come to Him just as we are, and are sorry for our sins, He will not cast us away. Jesus is good. He alone can forgive us for the bad and can wash away our sins. That is why He came and died on the cross so we can go free. You see, Jesus died in our place. We have all sinned and come short of His glory. He alone is good."

Chapter 12

Rejoicing in Heaven

There was great rejoicing over the small German Bible that Dilek and Lothar had found at the mill. Hans and Netta had both come from German descent and read German fluently.

"Now I can learn more verses," Dilek said eagerly. "I can learn more about my dear Lord and Saviour."

Hans and Netta both longed for the simple faith that Dilek so unfalteringly demonstrated in her life. She had no doubts, no reservations. When the precious Bible said something was true, it was! Dilek always believed!

Hans now read daily from the Bible, interpreting it into the Russian language for Dilek and Lothar to understand. Hans was gifted in bringing out the lessons simply. Then he led the family in prayer. Lothar was always included in these worship periods. At first he resented having to be there, but as time went on, he seemed to begin to enjoy them.

Dilek taught Lothar some hymns. His mellow voice was deepening. Their voices blended beautifully.

"If only we had some hymn books," Netta remarked one evening after they had sung together. Wistful tears slid down her cheek as she thought of those they used in her childhood home.

Her thoughts went to her family. None remained, as far as she knew, except Grandma and herself. What happy times they had had, when the country was free.

Lothar saw the tears. He knew the ache that accompanied them. He resolved that if at all possible, Netta would one day have hymn books again. He would skimp and save, beginning that very day, perhaps he would be able to locate some, somewhere.

Dilek walked to Netta and hugged her. "Mama, I love you dearly, and I too would like a hymn book, but I'm thankful we know songs of praise to sing from our hearts. I think your voice is beautiful. Oh, Mother, I do love you. Yet, I love my Jesus more." She whispered softly into Netta's ear, "You have done so much for me, but Jesus gave me a new life, and a new hope even though I do not deserve it. How I long to see Him someday."

Netta was touched by Dilek's sincere faith and confession. "Lord, help me to trust with childlike faith too," she prayed.

Dilek sat with rapt attention as the minister related the beautiful story of Philip and the Ethiopian eunuch.

"And Philip ran thither to him, and heard him read the prophet Esaias, and said, 'Understandest thou what thou readest?' " The minister paused, looking over the congregation.

"And the eunuch said, 'How can I, except some man should guide me?' And he desired Philip that he would come up and sit with him.

"The place of the scripture which he read was this; He was led as a sheep to the slaughter; and like a lamb dumb before his shearer, so opened he not his mouth.

" 'I pray thee,' asked Philip, 'of whom speaketh the prophet this, of himself or of some other man?'

"Then Philip began at the same scripture and preached unto him Jesus. God sent his only begotten son that whosoever believeth in him should not perish, but have everlasting life," the minister explained.

"He gave his life that we might have life. Neither is there salvation in any other; for there is none other name under heaven given among men, whereby we must be saved.

"Christ died on the cross, arose from the dead, and now sits at the right hand of God interceding for us," the minister continued.

"And as they went on their way, they came to a certain water and the eunuch said, 'See, here is water; what doth hinder me to be baptized?'

"And Philip said, 'If thou believest with all thine heart, thou mayest.'

"And he answered and said, 'I believe that Jesus Christ is the Son of God.'

"And he commanded the chariot to stand still; and they went down, both Philip and the eunuch, and he baptized him.

"Realizing it has been many years since there has been an opportunity for anyone to be baptized, we now give you that special privilege. We invite any true believer who can confess with the eunuch, 'I believe that Jesus Christ is the Son of God, to come forward, both young and old.'" The minister spoke with tears of love and sincerity.

Dilek rose to her feet. Surely Lothar could no longer hesitate after hearing such simple gospel truths. She walked to the front with some others. Fernella was among them.

Dilek knelt as she confessed her trust and acceptance of Jesus as the Son of God. She received baptism by pouring on of water. When she arose, she knew it was not the water that made her feel clean, but the blood of Jesus. How happy she felt, knowing her sins were washed away!

One shadow remained. Lothar, Papa, and Mama had not come forward for baptism. She trusted that concern to her Lord also. She had petitioned, and He would hear and answer when His time was right.

Hans and Netta spoke long that night. They read the Bible and searched for truths as never before.

"I feel as if I should have gone with my daughter," Netta said. "But I do want to be certain." The idea of baptism was still somewhat new to her.

"I am ready when the next privilege comes," Hans said. "I also thought I wanted to learn more first, but our child did not wait. She had faith."

188

A strange foreboding that her daughter was slipping fast from their need and care passed as a wave through Netta's heart. How quickly Dilek was growing up, almost to womanhood in stature! And, in maturity of mind and soul, she was more advanced than they, her parents.

Dilek could not keep her glorious happiness inside. Her joy was overflowing, and she got up each morning singing. She was a merry, happy girl from morning until night, helping someone else whenever she could.

Netta noticed that Dilek was gaining victory over her sudden fits of temper. Still she needed the encouragement that her Christian friends and family could give her. Truly the Lord had given her victory over many human weaknesses. She controlled her emotions well.

Lothar noticed the difference, too, and it added more disturbance to his already troubled conscience. Dilek lost no opportunity to speak to him about her Lord, yet always in a way that she might never offend him. She never nagged or tried to

189

force him to say he believed. His conversion meant too much to her; she wanted to be sure it would be genuine.

"That was a real storm last night," Dilek said to Lothar one morning. "At one time I would have been afraid, but I enjoyed watching the lightning. It was just as though God was using His light to see if He had washed all the earth and trees clean. And how clean it does smell this morning! There must not be a speck of dust left in any of the mountains or valleys."

Lothar stood amazed, speechless. He had been afraid at the fury of the storm and he was nearly a man, two years older than Dilek. "Yes, it was quite a storm," he finally muttered. "I wonder how much damage it might have done?"

If Lothar had expressed what was in his thoughts, he would have said he longed to have what Dilek had. Joy, assurance of sins forgiven, and a fearless disposition, just like the one dearest on earth to him. There was no one else like Dilek with whom to share his inner feelings. Somehow she always understood, even when he could not find the words to fully express himself.

"I'll go for water now," Dilek said, picking up the pail from the table. "It is such a wonderful morning for a walk. I feel as if I am walking with the lightness of those white clouds that cling to the mountain tops this morning. They look like huge fluffy towels, wiping dry the mountaintops. How beautiful God has made everything!"

Netta watched the tall slender girl swing the empty bucket, matching the mood and rhythm of her graceful steps. "She is so beautiful herself that it is best she does not realize it. Her free conscience and deep love for her Saviour glow on her face too. They make her even more beautiful."

Dilek stopped to see and listen to the gurgling water at the millstream. It flowed more rapidly than Dilek had ever seen it.

"The miller would grind his feed quickly this morning," she thought, "if the speed of the water had anything to do with it." She thought again of the German Bible they had found, and wondered what history might lie behind it.

"Oh, the great oak has blown over," Dilek said as she neared the home of little Roscoe. "The little Dear, I'm glad he has come to love hearing the Bible stories. He hasn't even been very naughty lately. There he is now, splashing in a puddle, which is not too hard to find this morning."

Dilek was about to call to him when her heart stood still. Roscoe was near the tree, ready to climb onto one of its branches. A high-powered electric line was coiled around it.

With a leap, she grabbed his arm and flung him away from the charged tree. She slipped in the same puddle Rosco had been playing in and fell sprawling.

Dilek did not scream. There was no sound at all. But the metal bucket she still held in her free hand touched the tree. Her body lurched, twisted into a ball, then lay still. Dilek had saved her little friend, but she was dead.

The minister that had been present only three weeks earlier to baptize Dilek, now returned to preach at her funeral.

"Her short life," he said, "speaks louder than any sermon I could give." He went on to speak comforting words about heaven.

Hans and Netta were grief stricken. "Why should we not be willing to let the Lord have her?" they asked one another. "He gave her to us to enjoy and learn from; now He took her to be with Himself. Blessed be the name of the Lord."

"Yes, she was still in the first joy of her Lord, like a bride espoused to her husband," Netta said, weeping. "We should be happy and rejoice with her that she could go to be with her Bridegroom so soon after she was baptized. She was a blossom in our home. She led us in spiritual truths. We must be ready to follow her when our call comes."

The death of Dilek crushed Lothar. He had nowhere to go to unload the stifling burden that threatened to crush him.

193

"Why, oh why does God take everything from me that is dear to me?" Lothar's sleep was restless as he asked that same question over and over again.

The answer came almost as plainly as if Dilek had said it just now, instead of weeks earlier. "You must love the Lord more than anything else, Lothar. He cannot and will not take second place in your heart!"

The message would not sink into his wounded heart. It bled with grief and loneliness. Tears wet his pillow until he finally fell asleep as the morning rays streaked across the eastern horizon.

Lothar dreamed of Dilek. He dreamed that Roscoe had pulled her into the puddle and had killed her intentionally with the wire. His feelings of resentment toward Roscoe deepened. Dilek was worth more than a hundred thousand bad boys like Roscoe, he thought.

When Lothar left for work that morning, he decided he could no longer stay at the Reimer home. Everything in and around the home reminded him of Dilek.

He would leave quietly, secretly that night. He was certain Hans and Netta would not agree to his leaving should they find out. Where he would go, he did not know and did not care.

He only wanted to get away. Away from Hans and Netta who always talked about God—God, who robbed him of all he ever had and gave him a tortured conscience besides. The further away from it all, he thought, the better off he would be.

Netta was shocked when she found that Lothar had gone. His clothes were gone too, so she knew he had no intentions of returning. Straightening his bed, she found a note crumbled under the pillow. "I wish to thank you, Onkel Hans and Tante Netta," she read through her tears, "for all you have done for me. You were very kind. I am not worth it all. I cannot stay to be reminded daily of Dilek. So, I say goodbye. Lothar."

Hans was grieved to learn of Lothar's decision. He had taken the boy as his own. Now that Dilek was no longer with them, they needed him more than ever.

"We will not try to seek him or bring him back. He will come on his own, if he wants to. It would be useless and senseless to try to force him to stay."

"We must pray for him more, Hans," Netta said softly. "Our Dilek prayed for him often and said the Lord would bring him to Himself in His own time. She trusted so. What will become of him?"

"Yes, Netta, we can pray and we will. I have a feeling it won't be too long, for where could he go? He has no one and not much money."

Netta visited Frau Rutini, hoping they had heard something from Lothar. "I thought perhaps now that Dilek is no longer with us, he might open up to Fernella. He needs someone."

"We did not see him, or even know that he had left, Netta. I am very sorry about it. We certainly will let you know if we hear anything."

Fernella loitered on the way home from school. She had helped the teacher with some art work for a school display, and now walked alone, slowly down the path leading home. Her mama would not be home from work yet anyway.

Fernella sadly missed Dilek. She rejoiced that she had accepted the Saviour and had been baptized the same day Dilek was. It had knit them into a deeper friendship than before.

"We are now sisters," Dilek had said afterwards, "sisters in the Lord." The two had embraced each other in true Christian love. They were no longer children, but lovely maidens.

Fernella came to a patch of woods that lay between them and the village. It was a wonderful place to explore, Dilek used to say.

"There is so much to remind me of Dilek," Fernella said aloud. "No wonder, she was such a dear." She walked on slowly, deep in thought. She bypassed the shady shortcut through the woods that she often used.

"Fernella!"

"Did someone call me?" Fernella stopped short. She looked to see if someone was hiding in the woods, but saw no

197

one. She began to walk on.

"Fernella!" This time the voice was more distinct.

"Who is it?" Fernella asked, stopping again.

"It's me," a voice said from behind a thick bush. Lothar stepped out into view.

Fernella gasped with relief. "Oh, Lothar, I am glad it was you. I was frightened at first. Do come along home with me. Mama will be so glad to see you. So will Hans, Netta and Grandma."

"Are you sure?" Lothar asked, still reluctant to come out from the shelter of the woods.

"I'm sure, Lothar. They have mourned for you as much as for Dilek."

"Oh, Fernella. I thought if I would go away, I could forget. It is useless. One can never forget a friend, no matter where you go. I have been so miserable with no one to speak to and no one to tell me what is right or wrong. Fernella, may I speak to you as I did to Dilek?"

"Certainly, Lothar. And I need you to talk to. I miss Dilek too.

"Fernella, Dilek was right. There is no real joy or peace or happiness, unless we—" Lothar could not continue. A tear slid down his cheek. He turned away to hide it.

"And, Fernella," Lothar finally said. "I settled the question before I came back, and now I want to be baptized too."

"Oh, I am so happy! Dilek often said she knew you would trust Jesus someday. She always prayed for you."

Lothar was deeply touched. "Will you pray for me too, Fernella, now that—?"

"Yes, I will," Fernella promised. "The minister will be here again this Sunday. Hans, Netta, and Mama want to be baptized. How wonderful that you will be here to join them!"

"I am not worthy, but I praise the Lord for His mercy. He has led me back in time." Lothar spoke with bowed head.

"There is great joy in heaven when a sinner repents and comes into the fold, Lothar. I think Dilek knows about this too. Let's thank God together," Fernella whispered softly, bowing her head.